WORLD OF
INFORMATION

Business Guide to

Japan

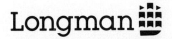

Longman

Longman Group Limited
Longman House, Burnt Mill, Harlow
Essex CM20 2JE, England
and Associated Companies throughout the world

First published 1986

ISBN 0 582 89337 2

Cover photograph: Japan National Tourist Organisation

Typesetting by Hart Talbot

Printed and bound in Great Britain
by Mackays of Chatham Ltd, Kent

Contents

☀ Introduction

Japan has risen from the ashes of the Second World War to support the second biggest economy in the world. In overall terms of gross national product, it is still less than half that of the United States, but in per capita terms at present rates it will surpass that of the USA before the end of the century. One estimate gives per capita income of the Japanese as more than $21,000 by the year 2000 as against $17,000 in the USA and less in Western Europe. The hard-working, hard-saving Japanese have piled up trade and balance of payment surpluses and are already taking over the role of 'banker to the world' as the USA becomes a net debtor. Japan is the only Far Eastern member of the Organisation for Economic Co-operation and Development, the club of rich industrial nations. The best expression of Japan's economic superiority can readily be seen all over the world in products 'Made in Japan', such as television sets, cameras, electronic equipment and cars. From being a producer of shoddy, cheap goods imitating Western products, by the 1980s Japan had shown that it has learned its lessons well: those Japanese products are the leaders, cheaper and of better quality than comparable goods offered by the once superior West.

At first sight Japan appears to have imbibed present American standards. In the last century the Meiji Restoration imposed a desire to learn from the West. Defeat by the USA in the Second World War and the subsequent American occupation and massive rehabilitation made sure that the economy and political life were modelled on those of the USA.

On the streets, signs in English, Western fast-food chains like McDonalds are spotted round the cities, pop music plays in bars and department stores and baseball is almost the national sport. Bankers and businessmen dress in Western suits neater and more regimented than any in the West. But underneath it all Japan also remains rooted in its own culture and history. It shares some things with its east Asian neighbours, notably China and Korea, but it has also developed them in unusual and often unique Japanese ways. The end product is a Japan convinced of its uniqueness and of the impossibility of any outsider really ever understanding it.

Key facts

Official title: Japan
Head of state: His Imperial Majesty Emperor Hirohito
Prime minister: Yasuhiro Nakasone
Ruling party: Liberal Democratic Party
Area: 377,781 sq km (several islands)
Population: 120m (1984)
Capital: Tokyo
Official language: Japanese
Currency: Yen (¥)
Exchange rate: Yen 213 per $ (Oct 1985)
GNP per capita: $7100 (1983)
GNP real growth: 5.8% (1984)
Unemployment: 2.6% (Aug 1985)
Inflation: 3.9% (1980–84)
Balance of trade: $49.6bn (year to Jul 1985)
Visitor numbers: 2m (1984)

World air distances

Below are distances in km from Tokyo for some of the world's major cities. They are not necessarily the shortest distances, but represent the most readily available flights.

Auckland	5487
Bangkok	4612
Beijing	2116
Delhi	5927
Dhaka	5343
Frankfurt	5933
Hong Kong	2903
Jakarta	5794
Karachi	6983
Kuala Lumpur	5354
London	6239
Manila	3016
Montreal	11,188
Moscow	4674
New York	6744
San Francisco	5135
Seoul	1194
Shanghai	1804
Singapore	5329
Sydney	4856
Taipei	2123
Vancouver	4687

International time in relation to Tokyo

Australia:	Eastern	+1
	Central	$+\frac{1}{2}$
	Western	−1
Austria		−8

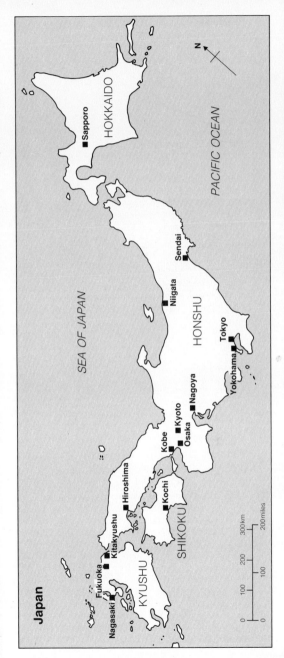

Japan

N

PACIFIC OCEAN

SEA OF JAPAN

HOKKAIDO

■ Sapporo

HONSHU

■ Sendai

■ Niigata

■ Tokyo

■ Yokohama

■ Nagoya

■ Kyoto

■ Osaka

■ Kobe

■ Hiroshima

Kitakyushu ■

Fukuoka ■

Nagasaki ■

KYUSHU

SHIKOKU

■ Kochi

0   100   200   300km

0   100   200miles

7

Bangladesh		−3
Belgium		−8
Canada:	Eastern	−14
	Pacific	−17
China		−1
Denmark		−8
France		−8
Germany		−8
Greece		−7
Hong Kong		−1
India		−3½
Indonesia:	Eastern	same
	Central	−1
	Western	−2
Italy		−8
Korea		same
Macau		−1
Malaysia		−1
Netherlands		−8
New Zealand		+3
Pakistan		−4
Papua New Guinea		+1
Philippines		−1
Singapore		−1
Sri Lanka		−3½
Switzerland		−8
Taiwan		−1
Thailand		−2
UK		−9
USA:	Eastern	−14
	Pacific	−17
USSR:	European	−6
	Asian	−5 to same

Allowances should be made for seasonal time changes, expecially during summer in Europe, North America and Australia, when time is advanced by one hour.

Population

Japan has a population of about 120m, ranking it the seventh most populous nation in the world. Its population density of 316 per sq km in 1983 is high. Of the total population 80 per cent lives in Honshu, itself 61 per cent of Japan's total area. Population growth slowed, with an annual growth of only 0.7 per cent during 1980-83. Total population is projected to be 128.1m in the year 2000. Life expectancy in Japan, at 74.2 years for men and 79.8 years for women, is the highest in the world. With the declining birth rate, by 2000 one in every five Japanese will be 60 years old or older. Tokyo has a population of around 12m. Osaka has about 8,640,000 and Yokohama around 2,770,000 people.

Getting there

Geography
Japan lies off the north-eastern coast of Asia and consists of four main islands – Hokkaido, Honshu, Shikoku and Kyushu, and thousands of smaller islands running in an arc from north (latitude 45°33'N) to south (latitude 24°25'N), with a total area of 377,781 sq km. Japan is mainly mountainous, with only 29 per cent of the national land area consisting of plains and basins. It has some 10 per cent of the world's active volcanoes, and its highest mountain, Mt Fuji (3776 m) is a dormant volcano.

Passports
All foreigners must have valid passports or internationally recognised travel documents.

Visas

Tourist
Period of stay is up to 90 days and 15 days for a transit visa holder.

Commercial
A commercial visa holder will usually be given a permit to stay for 180 days or more.

A number of countries have reciprocal visa exemption agreements with Japan. Citizens of the following countries are exempted from obtaining a visa as long as they do not intend to engage in any remunerative activity in Japan: Austria, Germany (FR), Republic of Ireland, Liechtenstein, Mexico, Switzerland and the UK.

Citizens of the following countries are exempted for up to 90 days with the same conditions: Argentina, Bangladesh, Belgium, Canada, Chile, Colombia, Costa Rica, Cyprus, Denmark, the Dominican Republic, El Salvador, Finland, France, Greece, Guatemala, Honduras, Iceland, Iran, Israel, Italy, Luxembourg, Malaysia, Malta, the Netherlands, Norway, Pakistan, Peru, Portugal, Lesotho, San Marino, Singapore, Spain, Surinam, Sweden, Tunisia, Turkey, Uruguay and Yugoslavia.

For New Zealand it is up to 30 days. All other nationals require visas.

Temporary landing without visa
Visas are not required of passengers of a commercial vessel or airline who are granted permits to land for

no more than 72 hours while the vessel or aircraft is in a Japanese port, or by passengers of a commercial vessel who are granted permits to land at one port for an overland tour of not more than 15 days and reboard the same vessel at another port while it is in Japan.

Within three months of landing, visitors who intend to extend their stay in Japan must apply to the mayor of the city or head of the town or village where they are staying for an alien registration certificate.

Visitors wishing to extend their stay must apply at an immigration office prior to the date of expiry of their visa.

Tokyo Immigration Office
1-3-1 Oote-machi, Chiyoda-ku, Tokyo (tel: 471.5111)

Osaka Immigration Office
2-31 Tani-machi, Higashi-ku (tel: 941.0771)

Yokohama Immigration Office
37-9 Yamashita-cho, Naka-ku (tel: 681.6801)

Visas should be obtained before departure from a Japanese embassy or consulate:

USA
Embassy of Japan
2520 Massachusetts Avenue NW, Washington, DC
(tel: 202.234.2266)

Consulate-General of Japan
1601 Post Street, San Francisco, California 94115
(tel: 415.921.8000)

Consulate-General of Japan
299 Park Avenue, New York, NY 10171
(tel: 212.371.8222)

Canada
Embassy of Japan
255 Sussex Drive, Ottawa, Ontario K1N 9E6
(tel: 613.236.8541)

Consulate-General of Japan
1210 Board of Trade Tower, 1177 W. Hastings Street,
Vancouver, BC V6E 2K9 (tel: 604.684.5868)

Consulat-Général du Japon
600 rue de la Gaucherière ouest, Suite 1785, Montreal,
Quebec H3B 4L8 (tel: 514.866.3429)

Europe
Japanische Botschaft
1040 Wien, Argentinierstrasse 21, Austria (tel: 65.97.71-8)

Ambassade du Japon
Avenue des Arts 58, 1040 Bruxelles, Belgium
(tel: 513.9200)

Embassy of Japan
Oslo Plads 14,2100 Copenhagen, Denmark
(tel: 01.26.33.11)

Embassy of Japan
Yrjonkatu 13,00120 Helsinki 12, Finland (tel: 644206)

Ambassade du Japon
7 Avenue Hoche, 75008 Paris, France (tel: 766.02.22)

Japanische Botschaft
Bundeskanzlerplatz, Bonn Center H1-701,5300 Bonn 1,
West Germany

Embassy of Japan
2-4 Messoghion Avenue, Athens Town Bldg, 21/floor
Athens, Greece (tel: 775.8101-3)

Embassy of Japan
22 Ailesbury Road, Dublin 4, Ireland (tel: 69.40.33)

Ambasciata del Giappone
Via Quintino Sella 60,00187 Roma, Italy (tel: 475.7151)

Ambassade du Japon
2 rue des Girondins, Luxembourg-Ville, Luxembourg
(tel: 448511)

Embassy of Japan
Park Veien 33-B, 0258, Oslo 2, Norway (tel: 02.56.48.94)

Embaixada do Japão
Avenida Fontes Pereira de Melo, 14-13-1098 Lisboa,
Portugal (tel: 562177)

Embajada del Japon
Calle de Joaquín Costa 29, 28002 Madrid, Spain
(tel: 262.55.46)

Embassy of Japan
Gardesgatan 10, 115 27 Stockholm, Sweden
(tel: 08.63.04.40)

Ambassade du Japon
43 Engestrasse, 3012 Berne, Switzerland
(tel: 031.24.08.11)

Embassy of Japan
43-46 Grosvenor Street, London W1X 0BA, UK
(tel: 01.493.6030)

Pacific
Embassy of Japan
112 Empire Circuit, Yarralumla, Canberra, ACT 2600,
Australia (tel: 733244)

Consulate-General of Japan
36th floor, 8-18 Bent Street, Sydney, NSW 2000,
Australia (tel: 02.231.3455)

Embassy of Japan
7th floor, Norwich Insurance House, 3-11 Hunter Street,
Wellington 1, New Zealand (tel: 731.540)

Embassy of Japan
4th and 5th floors, AMG House, Hunter Street, Port
Moresby, Papua New Guinea (tel: 211800)

Embassy of Japan
National Provident Fund Bldg, Mendana Avenue, Honiara,
Solomon Islands (tel: 22953)

Embassy of Japan
2nd floor, Dominion House, Suva, Fiji (tel: 25631)

Asia
Embassy of Japan
Plot No 110, Road No 27, Block A, Banani Model Town,
Dhaka 12, Bangladesh (tel: 600053)

Embassy of Japan
Lot 16464, Jalan Kebangsaan, Kampong Mabuhai, Bandar
Seri Bagawan, Brunei (tel: 29265)

Embassy of Japan
7 Ri Tan Road, Jian Guo Men Wai, Beijing People's
Republic of China (tel: 52.2361)

Consulate-General of Japan
25th floor, Bank of America Tower, Harcourt Road,
Central, Hong Kong (tel: 5.221184-8)

Embassy of Japan
Plot Nos 4 & 5, 50–G, Chanakyapuri, New Delhi, India
(tel: 604071-4)

Embassy of Japan
Jalan MH Thamrin 24, Jakarta, Indonesia (tel: 324308)

Embassy of Japan
18-11 Chunghak-dong, Chogro-ku, Seoul, Republic of
Korea (tel: 733.5626-8)

Embassy of Japan
11 Pesiaran Stonor, off Jalan Tun Razak, Kuala Lumpur,
Malaysia (tel: 438044)

Consulate-General of Japan
2 Biggs Road, Penang, Malaysia (tel: 24271)

Embassy of Japan
Plot No 53-70, Ramna 5/4, Diplomatic Enclave 1,
Islamabad, Pakistan (tel: 820181-4)

Embassy of Japan
375 Senator Gil J. Puyat Avenue, Makati, Metro Manila,
Philippines (tel: 818.9011-9)

Embassy of Japan
16 Nassim Road, Singapore (tel: 2358855-9)

Embassy of Japan
20 Gregory's Road, Colombo, Sri Lanka (tel: 93831-3)

Embassy of Japan
1674 New Petchburi Road, Bangkok 10310, Thailand
(tel: 252.6151-9)

Air access

Japan has several airports: Tokyo has Narita (inter-
national) and Haneda (domestic). Others are at
Fukuoka, Kagoshima, Komatsu (Kanazawa),
Kumamoto, Osaka, Nagasaki, Nagoya, Niigata,
Naha (Okinawa) and Chitose (Sapporo).

The main access is via Tokyo International Air-
port, located at Narita, 66 km from the city centre.
This means a time-consuming journey to or from
Narita, which can take half a day.

Probably the fastest means of getting to Narita is by taking the Keisei (private) Ueno Skyliner railway express (¥1490, child ¥750), which takes 60 minutes from Ueno Station in central Tokyo. There is a five-minute bus ride from the Narita railway station to the airport.

The other main way is to take a limousine bus from the Tokyo City Air Terminal (approximately one hour) or other city subcentres (aproximately one and a half hours). Bus fare is ¥2500 from TCAT and ¥2700 from Shinjuku, Ginza, Shiba, Akasaka, Ikebukuro and Shinagawa. Some buses do run to the main hotels, but frequently this service is limited. Bus journey times are frequently extended by traffic. It is wise to allow half an hour or more for delays. Narita gets clogged at certain times of day and waiting for a bus can take up to an hour.

Japan National Railways (JNR) runs limited express trains (¥2300) and rapid trains (¥1000) approximately a 70–80 minutes' ride from Tokyo Station. Airport buses then shuttle to the airport (¥350); approximate time 25 minutes.

Taxis are also available, but these are expensive, costing about ¥15,000 upwards. Both bus and taxi journeys are liable to delay in the frequently congested downtown Tokyo traffic. All passengers departing from Narita are subject to a Passenger Service Facility Charge of ¥2000 per adult and ¥1000 per child aged 2 – 12. There is no charge from any other airport in Japan.

At Osaka Airport taxis and limousines are available to Osaka city. The bus fare is ¥360, and the taxis range from ¥3000 up.

At Yokohama, limousines are available from Tokyo Narita Airport to/from Yokohama City Air Terminal for ¥3100. The approximate journey time is two hours.

Surface access

As Japan is an island country there is no possibility of driving to it. The country maintains excellent and busy ports such as Yokohama and Kobe, but these are used mainly for transporting goods, though cruise liners do use some ports.

Health

Visitors arriving from or via an area infected by cholera or yellow fever require the appropriate valid international certificate of vaccination.

Customs

Air travellers must declare their baggage orally, and each passenger must be cleared by a customs inspector. Japan maintains strict quarantine regulations against plant and animal diseases. Passengers with unaccompanied baggage must fill in two copies of a declaration form indicating their extra luggage, and have it verified at the time and place of entry so that their claim for free entry of their baggage can be supported.

Personal duty-free allowances: 400 cigarettes or 100 cigars or 500 gm of tobacco or an assortment not exceeding 500 gm; 3 bottles of liquor; 2 oz perfume; goods not exceeding ¥100,000 in value.

Prohibitions: narcotics; counterfeit, altered or imitation currency, notes, coins or other securities; pornographic or seditious material; weapons; articles infringing upon patent rights, copyright, etc.

Currency

Japan's currency is the yen.

Bank notes: ¥500, ¥1000, ¥5000, ¥10,000

Coins: ¥1, ¥5, ¥10, ¥50, ¥100, ¥500

In cities, foreign bank notes and travellers' cheques can be converted into yen at foreign exchange banks or licensed money changers. Unused local currency can be reconverted without limit. Any currency, personal ornaments or valuables can be brought in or taken out only with a customs officer's authorisation. Up to ¥5m can be taken out on departure. Credit cards such as American Express, VISA, Diners Club and MasterCard are acceptable at major establishments. However, personal cheques are not used as much as in the West so it is necessary always to have adequate cash when going out.

Exchange rates

	Currency unit	Yen per currency unit			
		1982 (Nov)	1983 (Nov)	1984 (Nov)	1985 (Nov)
Australia	dollar	244.63	213.91	210.64	138.47
Belgium	franc	523.20	428.18	394.40	394.57
Canada	dollar	204.77	188.79	185.91	145.78
China	yuan	127.25	117.97	88.22	63.22
France	franc	36.39	28.59	25.83	26.33
German FR	mark	102.85	87.01	79.11	80.32
Italy	lire	17.78	14.36	12.82	11.80
Netherlands	guilder	93.27	77.57	70.20	71.40
Sweden	kroner	34.20	29.44	27.87	26.42
Switzerland	franc	119.58	108.53	96.23	96.93
United Kingdom	pound	413.38	342.34	294.70	300.37
United States	dollar	233.00	237.00	231.00	254.00

Staying there

Climate

Japan has well-defined seasons. There are wide variations in temperatures between northern and southern areas. Spring is from March to May; average temperature 6.1°C to 20.6°C. Rainy season is from mid-June to mid-July. Summer is from June to August; average temperature 20°C to 27.9°C. September has several typhoons (heavy rains and strong winds). Autumn is from September to November; average temperature is 10.3°C to 23.9°C. Winter is from December to February; average temperature is from −5.1°C to 15.8°C. Rainfall is about 1000 to 2500 mm annually. Tokyo has an average 1942 hours of sunshine annually.

Social customs

The Japanese are a very polite people. Numerous courtesies are exchanged on simple meetings between Japanese, and although it is not expected that foreigners will follow these, a few simple courtesies will do much to smooth the way. Most Japanese businessmen today will shake hands, but a bow will do on introduction to their wives.

The exchange of business cards or *meishi* is universal in Japan. It helps to have your name in Japanese on the reverse. Remember always to exchange cards at the beginning of the first meeting. In Japan surnames are always given first and first names last. (Note that in this book persons are referred to by European usage.)

If you are invited to a Japanese home, it is customary to remove your shoes at the entrance and wear the house slippers provided. In traditional Japanese restaurants and homes meals are usually served round a low table, and you sit on the floor on cushions.

Gift giving is a very pleasant Japanese custom. Small items are to be found, pre-wrapped and suitable for all occasions at department stores or railway stations. One should get advice on what is appropriate for specific situations. Make sure not to give four of anything, as one of the forms of four, *shi,* has the same sound as the word for death.

Dress

In business life Japanese tend to dress formally with dark suits for men and suits and dresses for women. It is a good idea to dress accordingly. Certain hotels and restaurants impose a dress code.

Business hours
Government offices: 0900 – 1700, Mon to Fri; 0900 – 1200, Sat.
Other offices: 0900 – 1700, Mon to Fri; most offices close on Sat.
Note: Most Japanese work after hours, so if it is urgent try to call the direct line. The switchboard will probably shut at 1700 hours.
Banks: 0900 – 1500, Mon to Fri; 0900 – 1200, Sat.
Note: Banks close every second Sat of the month.
Shops: Department stores are usually open from 1000 to 1800, Mon to Fri and from 1000 to 1830, Sat and Sun.
Note: Department stores close one day a week; smaller shops are open 1000 – 2000.
Post office: 0900 – 1700, Mon to Fri; 0900 – 1230, Sat but financial department closed every second Sat of the month. The Central Post Office at Tokyo Station and every central post office in the area are open from 0900 – 1700, Sat and 0900 – 1230, Sun.

Public holidays
1 January	New Year's Day *(Ganjitsu)*
15 January	Coming of Age Day *(Seijin-no-hi)*
11 Febbruary	National Foundation Day *(Kenkoku-Kinenbi)*
21 March	Vernal Equinox Day *(Shunbun-no-hi)*
29 April	Birthday of the Emperor *(Tenno Tanjobi)*
3 May	Constitution Memorial Day *(Kenpoh Kinenbi)*
5 May	Children's Day *(Kodomo-no-hi)*
15 September	Respect for the Aged Day *(Keiroh-no-hi)*
23 Sepeptember	Autumn Equinox Day *(Shuubun-no-hi)*
10 October	Health and Sports Day *(Taiiku-no-hi)*
3 November	Culture Day *(Bunka-no-hi)*
23 November	Labour Thanksgiving Day *(Kinroh-Kansha-no-hi)*

When a national holiday falls on a Sun, the following Mon is a holiday.

Year end and New Year holiday season: 29 Dec to 3 Jan and adjacent weekends.

Golden week: 29 Apr to 5 May and adjacent weekends.

Bon festival season: a week around 15 Aug.

Language

Below is a list of common words and phrases.

Good morning	ohayoh (gozaimasu – this addition shows respect to older/important people)
Hello (daytime)	konnichiwa
Good evening	konbanwa
Goodbye	sayohnara
Goodnight	oyasuminasai
Thank you	arigatoh (gozaimasu)
Excuse me/sorry	sumimasen
It is wrong	chigaimasu
That's right	sohdesu
I don't understand	wakarimasen
I understand	wakarimashita
One	ichi *or* hitotsu
Two	ni *or* futatsu
Three	san *or* mittsu
four	shi *or* yottsu
five	go *or* itsutsu
six	roku *or* muttsu
seven	shichi *or* nana *or* nanatsu
eight	hachi *or* yattsu
nine	ku *or* kyuu *or* kokonotsu
ten	juu *or* toh
eleven	juu-ichi
twenty	ni-juu
thirty	san-juu
forty	shi-juu *or* yon-juu
fifty	go-juu
sixty	roku-juu
seventy	nana-juu *or* shichi-juu
eighty	hachi-juu
ninety	kyuu-juu
hundred	hyaku
thousand	sen *or* issen
5000	go-sen
10,000	ichi-man
100,000	juu-man
1,000,000	hyaku-man
yes	hai
no	iie
What time is it?	Nan-ji desuka.
hours, o'clock	–ji
Sunday	nichi-yohbi
Monday	getsu-yohbi
Tuesday	ka-yohbi
Wednesday	sui-yohbi
Thursday	moku-yohbi
Friday	kin-yohbi
Saturday	do-yohbi

holiday	kyuujitsu *or* yasumi
warm	atatakai
hot	atsui
cool	suzushii
cold	samui
where	doko *or* dochira
when	itsu
why	naze *or* dohshite
which	dore *or* dochira
who	donata *or* dare
How much (does this cost)?	(Kore wa) ikura desu ka.
how many?	ikutsu
please	dohzo
I	wata(ku)shi
you	anata
big/small	ookii/chiisai
quick/slow	hayai/osoi
early/late	hayai/osoi
cheap/expensive	yasui/takai
near/far	chikai/tooi
hot/cold	atsui/tsumetai
full/empty	ippai/kara
easy/difficult	yasashii/muzukashii
heavy/light	omoi/karui
open/shut	aite iru/shimatte iru
right/wrong	tadashii/machigatte iru
old/new	furui/atarashii
old/young	toshitotte iru/wakai
beautiful/ugly	utsukushii/minikui
good/bad	yoi/warui
at	-ni
on	-no ue-ni
in	-no naka-ni
to	-ni, -e
from	-kara
inside	-no naka-ni
outside	soto
up	-no ue-ni
down	shita-ni
before	-no mae-ni
after	-no ushiro-ni *(position) or* -no ato kara *(time delay)*
with/without	-to/-nashi ni
through	-o tootte
towards	-ni mukatte *or* -no hoh e
until	-made
during	-no aida
and	-to-
or	aruiwa *or* matawa
not	nai
nothing	nani-mo nai

none	hitotsu-mo nai
very	taihen
also	-mo *or* mata
soon	suguni
perhaps	tabun
here	koko
there	achira *or* asoko
now	ima
then	sono toki
Where can I get a taxi?	Doko de takushii ni noremasu ka.
Take me to . . .	. . . -ni tsurete itte kudasai.
this address	kono juusho
Go straight ahead	Massugu ni itte kudasai
Turn . . . at the next corner	Tsugi no magarikado o . . . ni magatte kudasai.
left/right	hidari e/migi e
Stop here please	Koko de tomatte kudasai.
lost and found office	ishitsubutsu-toriatsukaijo
bank	ginkoh
bookshop	honya
chemist	kusuriya
church	kyohkai
dentist	haisha
department store	depaato
doctor	isha
dry cleaners/laundry	kuriininguya/sentakuya
food/grocery store	shokuryohhinten
garden	teien *or* niwa
hairdresser	biyohin
hospital	byohin
liquor store	sakaya
museum	hakubutsukan, bijyutsukan
night club	naito kurabu
news-stand	shinbun-baiten, sutando
optician	meganeya
police station	kohban *or* keisatsu
post office	yuubinkyoku
restaurant	shokudoh *or* resutoran
shopping centre	shoppingu sentaa
toilets	otearai
yesterday	sakujitsu *or* kinoh
today	kyoh
tomorrow	asu *or* ashita
in the morning	gozen chuu
during the day	hiruma
in the afternoon	gogo
in the evening	ban
at night	yoru

month	tsuki
week	shuu
Jan	ichi-gatsu
Feb	ni-gatsu
Mar	san-gatsu
Apr	shi-gatsu
May	go-gatsu
June	roku-gatsu
July	shichi-gatsu
Aug	hachi-gatsu
Sep	ku-gatsu
Oct	juu-gatsu
Nov	juu-ichi-gatsu
Dec	juu-ni-gatsu
beer	biiru
bread	pan
butter	bataa
cheese	chiizu
coffee	koohii
dessert	dezaato
fish	sakana
fruit	kudamono
meat	niku
milk	miruku
mineral water	mineraru uootaa, mizu
oil	abura
pepper	koshoh
rice	gohan
salt	shio
soup	suupu
sugar	satoh
tea (Indian)	kohcha; *(Japanese)* ocha
vegetables	yasai
water	mizu
wine (from grapes)	budohshu, wain;
(Japanese, from rice)	sake
black	kuro
blue	ao
brown	chairo
crimson	makka
green	midori iro, ao
grey	hai iro
mauve	fuji iro
orange	daidai iro
pink	momo iro
red	aka
purple	murasaki iro
gold	kin iro
silver	gin iro
white	shiro
yellow	kiiro

Tipping

Tipping is not necessary in Japan. Hotels and most restaurants add on a 10–20 per cent service charge. Taxi drivers are not tipped, but hired car drivers should get ¥500 for a half-day excursion and ¥1000 for a full day. Porters should get ¥250 to ¥300 per piece of luggage at stations and ¥200 per piece at airports.

Hotels

Most major hotels are Westernised, with English-speaking staff who offer smooth service and efficient helpfulness. Some can provide business executive centres, help in arranging translation services, hired cars with chauffeurs and facilities for private receptions. Most provide facilities for direct-dial, long-distance calls individually accounted for in the bill, telex, facsimile, telegram and even post and courier services. First-class Western-style hotels will charge approximately ¥10,000 for a single room and ¥15,000 upwards for a twin, with an additional 10 per cent tax and 10–15 per cent service charge.

In Osaka first-class hotels will average ¥7000 upwards for a single room and ¥10,000 upwards for a twin, plus the 10 per cent tax and 10-15 per cent service charge.

In Yokohama first-class hotels range from ¥5000 upwards for a single room and ¥10,000 for a twin, plus the 10 per cent tax and 10–15 per cent service charge.

These hotels will generally have 24 hours' room service and excellent restaurants and cafés, with shopping arcades, health centres, etc. They will probably accept major credit cards.

All the hotels listed below are Westernised but the visitor may wish to spend a night or two at a *ryokan*, a Japanese inn. The main differences are that meals are usually served in the room; guests sleep on *futons* rather than bed; and a *yukata*, or cotton kimono, is provided for use in the room. The average price is ¥10,000 which includes two meals, tax and service charge.

Tokyo

Akasaka Prince
1 Kioi-cho, Chiyoda-ku, Tokyo 102
(tel: 234.1111; tx: 2324028) Banquet/meeting rooms, restaurants, gift shop, executive service centre, tour desk, medical, photo studio, beauty salon, outdoor parking.

Ginza Dai-Ichi
8-13-1 Ginza, Chuo-ku, Tokyo 104
(tel: 542.5311; tx: 2523714)

Ginza Tokyu
5-15-9 Ginza, Chuo-ku, Tokyo 104
(tel: 541.2411; tx: 2522601) Restaurants, conference
rooms, bookshop, travel agent, beauty salon, drug store.

Holiday Inn Tokyo
1-13-7 Hacchohbori, Chuo-ku Tokyo 104
(tel: 553.6161; tx: 2523748)

Grand Palace
1-1-1 Iidabashi, Chiyoda-ku, Tokyo 102
(tel: 264.1111; tx: 2322981) Restaurants, function rooms,
medical, business and travel services, shopping arcade, gift
shop, florist, bookstall, drug store, barber shop.

Ookura
2-10-4 Toranomon, Minato-ku, Tokyo 105
(tel: 582.0111; tx: 22790) Restaurants, convention and
banquet rooms, health club, executive service salon, private
museum.

Pacific Meridian
3-13-3 Takanawa, Minato-ku, Tokyo 108
(tel: 445.6711; tx: 22861)

Imperial
1-1-1 Uchisaiwai-cho, Chiyoda-ku, Tokyo 100
(tel: 504.1111; tx: 2222346) Banquet and convention
rooms, restaurants, business centre, shopping arcade,
bookstall, chemist, beauty salon.

Keio Plaza Intercontinental
2-2-1 Nishi-Shinjuku, Shinjuku-ku, Tokyo 160
(tel: 344.0111; tx: 26874) Banquet and function rooms,
restaurants, health service, shopping arcade.

Miyako Tokyo
1-1-50 Shiroganedai, Minato-ku, Tokyo 108
(tel: 447.3111; tx: 2423111) Function rooms, restaurants,
gymnasium, sauna, swimming pool, shopping arcade.

Palace
1-1-1 Marunouchi, Chiyoda-ku, Tokyo 100
(tel: 211.5211; tx: 2222580) Banquet and reception rooms,
restaurants, secretarial service, hire car, shopping arcade.

Shinbashi Dai-Ichi
1-2-6 Shinbashi, Minato-ku, Tokyo 105
(tel: 501.4411; tx: 2222233)

Takanawa Prince
3-13-1 Takanawa, Minato-ku, Tokyo 108
(tel: 447.1111; tx: 2423232) Convention service and rooms,
restaurants.

Century Hyatt Tokyo
2-7-2 Nishi-Shinjuku, Shinjuku-ku, Tokyo 160
(tel: 349.0111; tx: 29411) Banquet and reception rooms,
restaurants, discotheque, secretarial service, shops, pool.

New Ootani
4-1 Kioi-cho, Chiyoda-ku, Tokyo 102
(tel: 265.1111; tx: 24719) Largest hotel in Tokyo; banquet
facilities, restaurants, shopping arcade, secretarial service,
beauty salons, health club.

Tokyo Hilton International
6-6-2 Nishi-Shinjuku, Shinjuku-ku, Tokyo 160
(tel: 344.5111; tx: 2324515) Convention and reception
rooms, fitness centre, shopping arcade, tour desk, business
centre.

Tokyo Urashima
2-5-23 Harumi, Chuo-ku, Tokyo 100
(tel: 533.3111; tx: 2524297)

Tokyo Marunouchi
1-6-3 Marunouchi, Chiyoda-ku, Tokyo 108
(tel: 215.2151; tx: 2224655)

Tokyo Prince
3-3-1 Shiba Koen, Minato-ku, Tokyo 105
(tel: 432.1111; tx: 2422488) Conference rooms,
restaurants, shopping arcade, parking space.

Osaka
Ana Sheraton Osaka
1-3-1 Dojimahama, Kita-ku, Osaka 530
(tel: 347.1112; tx: 5236884) Convention rooms, indoor
pool and sauna, business centre, travel desk, barber shop
and beauty salon, restaurants.

Holiday Inn Nankai
28-1 Kyuzaemon-cho, Minami-ku, Osaka 542
(tel: 213.8281; tx: 5222939)

New Hankyu
1-1-35 Shibata, Kita-ku, Osaka 530
(tel: 372.5101; tx: 5233830) Convention facilities,
restaurants, photo studio, shopping, beauty salon,
bookstore, travel service, sauna, car hire, parking.

Nikko Osaka
7 Nishino-cho, Daihohji-cho, Minami-ku, Osaka 542
(tel: 244.1111; tx: 5227575) Function rooms, restaurants,
disco, beauty salon, florist, barber and shops.

Osaka Grand
2-3-18 Nakanoshima, Kita-ku, Osaka 530
(tel: 202.1212; tx: 5222301)

International Osaka
58 Hashizume-cho, Uchi-Honmachi, Higashi-ku,
Osaka 540
(tel: 941.2661; tx: 5293415) Function rooms, restaurants,
shopping centre.

Osaka Dai-Ichi
1-9-20 Umeda, Kita-ku, Osaka 530
(tel: 341.4411; tx: 5234423)

Osaka Terminal
3-1-1 Umeda, Kita-ku, Osaka 530
(tel: 344.1235, tx: 5233738) Banquet and conference
rooms, restaurants.

Osaka Tokyu
7-20 Chaya-machi, Kita-ku, Osaka 530
(tel: 373.2411; tx: 5236751) Restaurant, travel agent,
sundries shop, swimming pool.

Royal
5-3-68, Nakanoshima, Kita-ku, Osaka 530
(tel: 448.1121; tx: 63350) Banquet rooms, restaurant,
swimming pool, health club, shopping centre, cultural
school, babysitting.

Plaza
2-2-49 Ooyodo-minami, Ooyodo-ku, Osaka 531
(tel: 453.1111; tx: 5245557) Function rooms, restaurants,
shopping arcade, swimming pool, airlines counter, 450-car
garage.

Toyo
3-16-19 Toyosaki, Ooyodo-ku, Osaka 531
(tel: 372.8181; tx: 5233886) Function rooms, restaurants,
sauna, shopping arcade, photo studio.

Yokohama
New Grand
10 Yamashita-cho, Naka-ku, Yokohama 231
(tel: 681 1841; tx: 3823411)

Sunroute Yokohama
2-9-1 Kita-Saiwai-cho, Nishi-ku, Yokohama 220
(tel: 314.3111; tx: 3823632)

Satellite Yokohama
76 Yamashita-cho, Naka-ku, Yokohama 231
(tel: 641.8571; tx: 3822027)

Yokohama
6-1 Yamashita-cho, Naka-ku, Yokohama 231
(tel: 662.1321; tx: 3822061)

Yokohama Tokyu
1-1-12 Minami-Saiwai-cho, Nishi-ku, Yokohama 219
(tel: 311.1682; tx: 3822264)

Restaurants
Japan offers a bewildering selection of food. Here is
a brief guide to the different kinds of Japanese cooking.
   Japanese seafood specialities include
sushi: delicate cuts of raw fish wrapped in vinegared
rice and seaweed;
sashimi: bite-sized pieces of sliced, fresh, raw seafood served with soy sauce and Japanese mustard;
tenpura: fresh fish, vegetables dipped in batter and
briefly deep-fried;
sukiyaki: slices of raw beef bean-curd, vegetables
and noodles cooked in front of you with sweetened
soy sauce. You help yourself from the dish and dip
the pieces into raw egg yolk (dishes are individually
served);
yakitori: skewered pieces of chicken, duck or quail
dipped in soy sauce and cooked over an open char-
coal grill;
sumibiyaki: charcoal-broiled steaks;
teppan yaki: meat and vegetables grilled on a table-
top iron plate.

Most Japanese restaurants overcome the problem of the language barrier by laying out selections of dishes, made entirely of wax, in showcases, so that all you do is point to the one you fancy.

Sake is a heady rice wine and is drunk usually warm from small porcelain cups. Beer is also popular in Japan. The main brands are Asahi, Kirin, Sapporo and Suntory.

Japan also boasts Western-style cuisine and a number of very good restaurants that compare very favourably internationally. American Express, Diners Club, MasterCard and VISA are usually accepted in the bigger, more expensive restaurants, but it is wise to check beforehand and carry cash in case they are not.

Tokyo

JAPANESE CUISINE
Sushi
Shintaro
1-51 Kanda Jimbo-cho, Chiyoda-ku, Tokyo
(tel: 293.0709), 1100 – 2200

Shabu shabu
Hassan
6-1-20 Roppongi, Minato-ku, Tokyo
(tel: 403.9112), 1130–2330

Shabu Zen
5-17 Roppongi, Minato-ku, Tokyo
(tel: 585.5388), reservations required, 1700–2400

Tenpura
Ten-ichi Tenpura
6-6-5 Ginza, Chuo-ku, Tokyo
(tel: 571,1949), many branches, 1130 – 2130

Teppan yaki
Hama
7-2-10 Roppongi, Minato-ku, Tokyo
(tel: 403.1717), steak house, 1130 – 1400 and 1700 – 0200,
closed on Sun

GENERAL
Hisago
1-5-15 Hirakawa-cho, Chiyoda-ku, Tokyo
(tel: 261.8752), various Japanese cuisines, 1130 – 1500 and
1630 – 2200

FOR SPECIAL OCCASIONS
L'Orangerie
Hanae Mori Bldg, 3-6-1 Kita Aoyama, Minato-ku, Tokyo
(tel: 407.7461)

Maxim's
Sony Bldg, Ginza, Chuo-ku, Tokyo
(tel: 571.3621)

Chez Inno
11-2-3 Kyobashi, Chuo-ku, Tokyo
(tel: 274.2020)

The bigger first-class hotels have excellent restaurants, but apart from those there are many many more in the city. All varieties of national cuisine are represented – from Greek to Swiss, including American, Chinese, French, Hungarian, Indian, Indonesian, Italian, Korean, Mexican, Middle Eastern, Spanish, Taiwanese to Thai at last count.

Osaka

There is a saying that Osaka people spend their money on food until they go bankrupt. Naturally, there are dozens of eating places. There are also some Osaka delicacies: *Osaka-zushi* is characterised by its square shape with vinegared fish or broiled eel spread on top of rice; *fugu* (globe-fish dishes) is eaten pot-boiled or as *sashimi; takoyaki* is a small, round, wheat-flour dumpling with pieces of octopus and vegetables in it.

These are some of the many Japanese restaurants in Osaka:

Benkey
In the Hotel Nikko, 7 Nishino-cho, Daihohji-cho, Minami-ku, Osaka
(tel: 244.1111)

Miniu
Bingo-cho 5-chome, Higashi-ku, Osaka
(tel: 261.7241)

Minokichi
specialising in *Shabu Shabu,* Yagi Bldg, Minami-cho, Kitarochi 2-chrome, Higashi-ku, Osaka
(tel: 262.4185)

Yokohama

Some of the Japanese restaurants in the city are listed below:

Misago Zushi
specialising in *sushi,* 1-2-5 Yamat-cho, Naka-ku, Yokohama
(tel: 621.3353)

Serina
where *shabu shabu* is a speciality, 4-4-5 Sumiyoshi-cho, Naka-ku, Yokohama
(tel: 681.2727)

Araiya
specialises in *sukiyaki,* 2-1-7 Akebono-cho, Naka-ku, Yokohama
(tel: 251.5001)

Transport

Tokyo and other major Japanese cities are well served by public transport systems. Tokyo itself and Osaka, Kobe, Kyoto, Nagoya and Yokohama, Fukuoka (Hakata) and Sapporo all have underground subway systems, probably the quickest way of crossing the cities, as well as the Japan National Railway (JNR) lines. There are several problems for foreigners using the railways. The subways get very congested at rush hours and some of the stations are so big that it is possible to get lost in finding the exit nearest to your destination. JNR is not always helpful in supplying information in English. The vast Shinjuku Station in Tokyo is notorious in this respect.

Taxis
Going by taxi has its own difficulties. Taxi drivers are generally honest but few of them understand English, so it is well to carry a card with your destination written in Japanese. The other problem with taxis is the rush-hour traffic congestion which can lengthen short journeys. Taxi fares in Tokyo start from about ¥470 for the first two km and ¥80 for each additional 370 m after that. The time charge in slow traffic is ¥80 for every $2\frac{1}{2}$ minutes. A late-night charge of 20 per cent operates from 2300 to 0500. Toll charges on the expressway cost an extra ¥500 for small cars and ¥1000 for larger ones. Taxi stands are usually found in front of big hotels and railway stations. There are also radio taxis which charge from the time that they are engaged by dispatcher.

Subways
Minimum fare is ¥120 for private lines and ¥140 for Toei lines. Stations have automatic vendors where you select your ticket and get change. Tickets must be punched as you go through and must be turned in at the end of the ride. There are ten lines in the Tokyo subway system. They operate from about 0500 to just before midnight.

The Osaka subway system has six lines. These intersect with JNR lines and private railways, and in the city centre each line has it own terminal.

Yokohama has only one subway line. Private and JNR lines operate through the city.

Japan National Railway trains (Kokuden)
JNR operates electric trains in and through Tokyo. The Yamanote-sen line circles Tokyo, stopping at all subcentres. The Chuo-sen line goes from Tokyo Station to Shinjuku and beyond, stopping only three times. The Sohbu-sen services the stops between Shinjuku and Ochanomizu. There are also a number of private lines linking Tokyo to other cities, but these are sign-posted only in Japanese.

Shinkansen (bullet trains) are super-express lines operated by JNR, and there are only three: the original Tohkaido-Sanyo line from Tokyo plus the

Tohoku and Johetsu lines from Ueno. The Tohkaido–Sanyo *Shinkansen* links Tokyo Station with Nagoya, Kyoto, Osaka, Kobe, Okayama, Hiroshima, Shimonoseki and Fukuoka (Hakata). Then there is the Tohhoku *Shinkansen* from Ueno to Sendai and Morioka in northern Honshu. Third is the Johetsu *Shinkansen,* also from Ueno across Honshu to the Sea of Japan and Niigata. There are other ordinary limited express and sleeper express trains running between most major cities.

The Japan Rail Pass, available only to foreign tourists, is for 7, 14 and 21 days, and allows unlimited travel on these expresses for these periods, including express surcharges and reserved seat charges. They cost ¥21,000, ¥33,000 and ¥44,000 respectively, and can be purchased only outside Japan.

Ferries
These ply regularly from Tokyo and Osaka to Okinawa, Kagoshima to Okinawa, and Tokyo to Kushiro in Hokkaido. Hokkaido ferries ply between Aomori and Hakodate. There are other services to Honshu, Shikoku and Kyushu. There is also a regular ferry service from Pusan in South Korea to Shimonoseki.

Domestic air services
Japan Air Lines (JAL) operates only on main route services from Haneda Airport to Sapporo, Osaka, Fukuoka and Okinawa. All Nippon Airways (ANA) also flies on trunk and local routes. Toa Domestic Airlines (TDA) flies only on local line operations.

Car hire
There are several car rental bureaux in Japan. A visitor requires an international driving licence. The average rate for 24 hours with unlimited mileage but not including petrol is ¥7500 for a subcompact; ¥12,200 for a compact, ¥15,000 for an intermediate and ¥21,500 for a standard size car. Be warned that signs are in Japanese and driving is on the left side of the road. Insurance is approximately ¥1100 per day. Usually no deposit is required.

Tokyo
Avis International Ltd (tel: 502.2969)
Hertz Japan Ltd (tel: 496.0919)
Japan Rent a Car Service (Haneda) (tel: 747.8785)
Mitsubishi Auto Lease (tel: 572.5651)
Toyota Rent a Car Service (tel: 264.2834)
Osaka
Nippon Rent a Car (tel: 373.2652)
Nissan Rent a Car (tel: 372.0281)
Toyota Rent a Car (tel: 372.5480)
Mazda Rent a Car (tel: 361.3961)

What to buy

Traditional purchases would consist of the local handicrafts, especially the lacquerware, wood-block prints, silk, porcelain and pottery, cloissonné, washi paper, screens, folkcraft fans, kimonos, dolls and antiques. These are to be found in any number of speciality shops, including the tax-free emporia where one can also buy pearls, jewellery, cameras, electronic goods and watches. Hotel arcades have many shops, but it is a good idea to get out of the hotels for the variety of goods and variety of prices too.

Commodity tax is imposed on some luxury goods, from which foreigners are exempt. When buying tax-free goods, a foreigner must hand over his passport so that a record of the purchase's exemption from commodity tax is attached. Prices in commodity-tax-free shops should be compared with those of discount shops, which may be favourable.

Tokyo: The main shopping area is Ginza, where there are various department stores, but there are also large shopping centres in Shibuya, Shinjuku and Ikebukuro. Akihabara is noted for electric and electronic appliances available at discounts and tax-deducted prices.

Osaka: The best shopping area is Shinsaibashi, around Umeda Station with underground as well as upper level shopping complexes. Nanba and Tennohji are also popular with shoppers. Nipponbashi-suji is the electrical goods area.

Yokohama: Isezaki Mall is the main shopping street in Yokohama. Motomachi offers up-market fashion, and the area of Yokohama Station has the biggest and busiest shopping area in the city.

What to see and do in Tokyo

Sightseeing

The *Imperial Palace* which holds some remains of old Edo castle is a favourite. The Emperor's palace lies inside thickly wooded grounds and is only partly opened at New Year and on the Emperor's birthday. *Kitanomaru Park* lies north-west of the east garden of the Imperial Palace and encloses the *Nippon Budohkan Hall, the National Museum of Modern Art* and the *Crafts Gallery.* To the west is *Chidorigafuchi Park,* famous for its cherry blossoms in season. There are also a number of large parks worth visiting, for example *Shinjuku-Gyoen, Hibiya Park, Yoyogi Park, Kohrakuen Park, Rikugien Park* and *Ueno Park.*

The Meiji Shrine at Harajuku is dedicated to the Emperor Meiji and his empress, Shotoku. It stands in wooded grounds with a famous iris garden.

Ginza is the nation's most famous shopping district, with restaurants, nightclubs and coffee bars and hotels rubbing shoulders with long-established department stores and new, up-market, high-fashion boutiques.

Ueno contains most of old Tokyo. There are many museums here including the *Tokyo Bunka Kaikan Hall, Metropolitan Art Museum, National Museum of Western Art, Tokyo National Musuem, National Science Museum,* and *Ueno-no-mori Art Musuem. Ueno Zoo,* the largest in the country, has the only pandas in Japan. There is also a folklore museum, *Shitamachi Fuuzoku Shiryohkan,* which recreates the life of the old downtown districts. *Asakusa Kannon Temple (Sensohji),* in Asakusa, was founded in AD645. Behind the temple is the *Asakusa Shrine,* which is the home of the Sanja festival.

· *Tokyo Disneyland* is located at Urayasu, Chiba Prefecture. You can get to it from either Nihonbashi or Otemachi stations by subway Tozai line to Urayasu (a 15-minute ride). Then it takes five minutes to a special shuttle bus yard for a bus ride (¥200 adults, ¥100 children) of 20 minutes. There are also direct shuttle buses from Tokyo Station taking about 35 minutes. Tokyo Disneyland is open from 0900 to 1900 on weekdays; on weekends it closes at 2000.

Museums

Museums in Tokyo worth a visit:

Idemitsu Musuem of Art in Ginza has a private collection of fine arts and crafts from Japan and the Far East.

Japanese Sword Museum in Shinjuku houses masterpieces of Japanese swordsmiths.

Paper Museum in front of Ohji Station has a unique collection of Japanese paper, paper products and equipment. It is closed on national holidays.

Riccar Art Musuem at Ginza specialises in *ukiyoe* wood-block prints.

Ukiyoe Ohta Memorial Museum of Art in Harajuku has a large collection of wood-block prints.

Theatre

Japanese theatre is a special cultural experience. Theatre today can be divided by type into *noh,* dance drama; *kyohgen,* short comic plays; *kabuki,* dance-drama mirroring manners and customs of the Edo period; *bunraku,* sophisticated puppet theatre featuring large puppets, narrators and musicians; *shinpa,* (new school) drama depicting contemporary Japan in the Meiji era in a naturalistic style; *shinkokugeki* (new national theatre) a popular presentation of period dramas; *shingeki* (new theatre) reflecting Japan's social conditions during the modernisation process.

Kabuki is performed at the National Theatre and Kabukiza Theatre in Tokyo. *Bunraku* is performed at the small hall of the National Theatre three times a year for 10 to 15 days. *Noh* plays are performed in several Nohgakudoh in Tokyo and in the National Noh Theatre. The *Takarazuka Revue* comes from Takarazuka near Osaka. These all-girl troupes present colourful musical revues at the Tokyo Takarazuka Theatre.

Cultural institutions

Other famous Japanese cultural institutions are the tea ceremony and *ikebana* (flower arranging). The tea ceremony can be observed at Sadho Bunka Shinkohkai and Tea Ceremony Service Centre near Ikebukuro. Tea ceremonies are also conducted in the Hotel Okura, the New Otani and Imperial Hotel in Tokyo.

The Ohara School of Ikebana holds two-hour courses on flower arranging. Another school is the Sogetsu School.

There are also classes in *origami,* paper folding, Japanese cooking and doll-making.

Sumoh wrestling is also typically Japanese. Professional *sumoh* has a history of centuries. Three annual tournaments of the total six are held in Tokyo at the Kokugikan Sumoh Hall in Jan, May and Sep.

Short tours

Japan Tourist Office also recommends a number of day tours or short trips to surrounding areas, including visits to Kyoto, Nara, Nikko, Hakone, Mt Fuji and Kamakura.

What to see and do in other major centres

Osaka

The *Ohatsu Tenjin Shrine* near Umeda Station is the setting of the famous story *Sonezaki Shinju* (lovers' suicide at Sonezaki).

Osaka Castle was built by Hideyoshi Toyotomi in the late sixteenth century. Inside is a historical museum. Outside the castle tower is the *City Museum* illustrating the history and culture of the city.

The *Mint Museum* exhibits Japanese and foreign coins and shows the history of the mint.

Tennohji Park has a botanical garden, zoo, library, art museum and a Japanese garden.

Shitennohji Temple, founded in AD593, is the oldest national temple in Japan, though the temple buildings have been often reconstructed after repeated fires.

The Museum of Oriental Ceramics in Nakano-shima Park displays priceless Chinese and Korean ceramics. *Nakanoshima Park* is the oldest park in Osaka, and lies at the eastern end of Nakanoshima, the administrative centre of Osaka situated on an island. The *Expo Memorial Park* lies outside Osaka city centre but is worth a trip. It lies on the former site of the 1970 World Exposition. It contains a Japanese garden, the Expo commemoration hall, *National Museum of Ethnology, Japan Folk Crafts Museum* and *Expo Land,* an amusement park for children.

The Sumiyoshi Shrine also lies outside Osaka city centre. It is said to have been founded by the Empress Jingu in the third century. The buildings have a particular style called *sumiyoshi-zukuri* and are designated a national treasure.

Yokohama

The *Silk Centre* contains the silk museum, showing the processes of silk manufacture and silk products. *Yamashita Park* was laid out in 1930, but is the oldest park in Japan to have been built alongside a beach. *Marine Tower* stands in Yamashita Park, and rises to 113 m. The top is used as a lighthouse. There is also a science museum in the tower. The *Iseyama Shrine* is worshipped by citizens as the guardian of Yokohama. It has a *torii* gate, which stands 10 m high, made of Japanese cypress.

Sankeien Garden is a Japanese landscape garden covering 19 ha. It contains a three-storey pagoda, the *Rinshunkaku Hall* and the *Chohshuukaku Pavilion* (tea-ceremony house).

Sohjiji Temple is one of the two headquarters of the Sohtoh sect of Zen Buddhism.

Tourist Information Centres

The Tourist Information Centres located in the various cities are enormously helpful in supplying maps and information and in recommending things to see and do. The staff speak various languages. They can also arrange a visit to a Japanese home so that visitors can see how the Japanese live.

Tokyo Tourist Information Centre
1-6-6 Yuuraku-cho, Chiyoda-ku, Tokyo
(tel: 502.1461)) also at Narita (tel: 0476.32.8711)

Osaka Tourist Information Centre
Higashiguchi, JNR Osaka Station, 3-1-1 Umeda, Kita-ku, Osaka (tel: 345.2189)

Yokohama Municipal Tourist Association
Silk Centre Bldg, 1 Yamashita-cho, Naka-ku, Yokohama (tel: 641.5824)

▥ History and government

Summary of history

According to Japanese mythology the country was founded by the descendant of the sun goddess Amaterasu-Oomikami, who pacified the Yamato region and created and ascended the imperial throne as Emperor Jinmu. This mythology places Jinmu's creation before there are firm historical dates for the foundation of the Japanese state. The northern part of the Japanese islands were originally occupied by the Ainu, who were conquered by mongoloid migrants who reached Japan by the Korean peninsula. Only about 20,000 Ainu remain today. The historical foundation of present-day Japan with an emperor dates from the end of the sixth century AD and with the Yamato court based around present-day Nara. At this time Japan, Korea and China had strong links. Refugees from troubled Korea and china came to Japan and brought products of their advanced technology, such as silk-worm cultivation, weaving, carpentry and forging of metal. China provided Japan with its writing system, the teachings of Confucius and Mencius and Buddhism. Japan at various times tried to extend its rule, notably over Korea. The Mongols of Ghenghis Khan invaded Japan, but were defeated as much by bad weather as by the Japanese fleet.

Inside Japan, stability was provided by the emperor regarded as the supreme deity in the Shinto pantheon; but the emperor's political power was rarely secure. From the latter half of the ninth century until the twelfth century the Fujiwara family was powerful, holding the office of *kanpaku* (literally meaning 'regent' but sometimes translated as 'civil dictator').

By the twelfth century, however, powerful regional families had sprung up in the countryside protected by groups of warriors or *samurai*. The two most powerful clans were the Taira and the Minamoto. Clashes between them brought victory by the Taira who seized power from the Fujiwaras. But the victory was short-lived, and the Minamoto eventually achieved revenge by destroying the Taira clan. In 1185 the Minamoto established the shogunate based at Kamakura, separate from the imperial court at Kyoto. Attempts by the disgruntled imperial forces to wrest back control failed, and the shogunate extended its power throughout Japan. The Kamakura shogunate defended Japan from two attempted Mongol invasions in 1274 and 1281. But then discontent among the *samurai* helped to weaken the shogunate and made way for a return to direct imperial rule. This too was short-lived, lasting a mere two years before the *samurai* resented attempts to impose new taxes. For the next 300 years civil war rumbled through Japan. In 1392 the Ashikaga shogunate established its sway in Kyoto, but its authority was not absolute and warriors with strong support began to emerge as feudal lords or *daimyo*. Power struggles between these *daimyo* intensified and developed into the *sengoku-jidai* or age of the warring states.

Out of this chaos, during which Kyoto was left in ashes, a succession of three powerful leaders – Nobunaga Oda, Hideyoshi Toyotomi and Ieyasu Tokugawa – emerged to unify Japan. Nobunaga rose from the Nagoya area to defeat other *daimyo* and destroy the Ashikaga shogunate, but he was then attacked by a retainer and forced to commit suicide. Hideyoshi, originally from a poor peasant family in Nagoya, destroyed the upstart retainer, built Osaka Castle as his base and by 1590 unified the country. He did not become *shogun,* only *kanpaku.* He surveyed the country and its productive capacity and took weapons from the common people. Hideyoshi traded with the Europeans who first came to Japan in 1543 when a Portuguese ship was blown aground at Tanegashima, a small island south of Kyuushuu. But Hideyoshi outlawed Christianity, which had followed the Europeans when Francis Xavier landed in Kagoshima in 1549. The dictator feared that Christianity would become the basis for a challenge to his authority. His final years were marred by an attempted invasion of Korea, which failed when the Japanese forces were withdrawn on Hideyoshi's death in 1598.

Ieyasu Tokugawa, who eventually emerged with power, had co-operated with Hideyoshi in pacifying Japan. Ordered to move his domain to the Kanto region, he set up headquarters at Edo Castle. In 1600 Tokugawa defeated Hideyoshi's son and in 1603 was able to establish himself as *shogun* with headquarters at Edo (present-day Tokyo). He developed a centralised bureaucracy and established a government system which lasted 264 years. Although encouraging initially to foreign trade, he and his successors closed the doors of Japan except to the Dutch, who were allowed to land one ship a year near Nagasaki.

In the middle of the nineteenth century, isolation was ended by the Western powers. Rivalry between

Russia and the United States sparked off the attempts to force Japan open. Russian ships had been prowling the waters around Japan, but when Commodore Matthew Perry entered Edo Bay on 8 July 1853 the Russians were distracted by the forthcoming Crimea War. Perry presented his demands, and in March 1854 Japan signed a treaty of amity and commerce with the USA. The arrival of the foreign powers gave the final push to the shogunate system, which was already weakened from within by financial problems, by the crumbling of the old feudal order and by the resentment of the lower *samurai* class, especially from Chohsyu and Satsuma. In 1867 and 1868 the opponents united. Unlike other revolutions which overthrew traditional monarchy, in Japan the emperor was restored to power in the Meiji Restoration *(meiji* means 'enlightenment').

Newly opened Japan showed how quickly it responded to the abolition of feudalism and the introduction of new learning and technology from the West. Universal education helped commerce and industry. By the turn of the century Japan was a growing force in international politics. In 1876 it forced Korea to open up to foreign trade, and thereby incurred the hostility of China, which regarded Korea as one of its tributory states. By 1912, when the Emperor Meiji (Mutsuhito) died, Japan had defeated the Russians, annexed Korea and forced China to cede Tiawan and the Pescadores Islands to it.

As the twentieth century wore on, Japan began to show extreme nationalism. It had sided with Britain against Germany in the First World War, and had been awarded all the German concessions in Shantung and a League of Nations mandate over the German Pacific colonies. Apologists say that one major cause of the nationalism was the Great Depression in the United States, which spread to Japan and caused great hardship. This provoked widespread dissatisfaction with the traditional leadership and paved the way for nationalists who wanted to use dictatorial powers to reform the country. Within this group the military increasingly held sway. In 1932 Prime Minister Tsuyoshi Inukai was shot dead by military and other right-wing figures, and four years later young officers assassinated other leading politicians. These nationalists believed that their country's unique spirit would ensure them victory over any enemy.

Japanese troops originally sent in the late 1920s to impede Chiang Kai-shek's efforts to unify the country had begun to carve up China. On 7 December 1941 Japan attacked Pearl Harbor to begin the Pacific War. Virtually simultaneous attacks on Malaya, Burma, the Philippines and the Dutch East Indies (Indonesia) seemed at first to prove the invincibility of the Japanese spirit. But then the Allied forces, unprepared for the Japanese aggression and preoccupied with their own war, began to counterattack. By 1945 the Americans had seized Okinawa and were bombing the Japanese islands. It looked as if it might be a hand-to-hand fight for victory, but then President Harry Truman decided to use the atomic weapon. Atomic bombs were dropped on Hiroshima on 6 August 1945 and on Nagasaki three days later. On 14 August Japan signalled it was prepared to surrender, and the next day the Emperor went on the radio to tell his people of Japan's surrender.

US General Douglas MacArthur became Supreme Commander of the Allied powers occupying Japan. MacArthur set up war crimes trials that saw former Prime Minister General Tojo, five other military leaders and former Prime Minister Kohki Hirota hanged. About 180,000 officials were purged and a new democratic constitution promulgated. Reforms were also carried out in education, land and the economic structure with the dismantling of the *zaibatsu*, the huge financial and industrial combines. In 1948 the Allied powers began transferring decision-making to a Japanese government. In 1951 Japan recognised Korea's independence and renounced claims to Taiwan, the Pescadores, southern Sakhalin and other territories that it once occupied. And on 28 April 1952 Japan regained its independence.

Important dates in Japanese history

600 BC	Mythical date of the accession of the first emperor, Jinmu
AD 300–645	*Yamato Period*
552 or 538	Buddhism introduced from Korea
710–784	*Nara Period*
794–1185	*Heian Period*
894	The practice of sending envoys to China abolished
995–1027	Fujiwara-no-Michinaga supreme
1169–81	Taira no Kiyomori supreme
1180–85	Genpei War (between the Minamoto and the Taira)
1185–1333	*Kamakura Period*
1192	Kamakura shogunate founded
1274	First Mongol invasion
1281	Second Mongol invasion
1333	Fall of the Kamakura shogunate
1338–1573	*Muromachi* (or *Ashikaga*) *Period*

1543	Portuguese land on Tanegashima Island
1549	Francis Xavier arrives in Japan
1568–1600	*Azuchi-Momoyama Period*
1568	Nobunaga Oda seizes Kyoto
1582	Nobunaga assassinated
1585	Hideyoshi Toyotomi appointed *kanpaku*
1592	*Hideyoshi's first invasion of Korea*
1600—1868	*Edo* (or *Tokugawa*) *Period*
1603	Founding of Tokugawa shogunate
1615	Fall of Toyotomi family
1639	*Sakoku-rei* (isolation order) promulgated
1853	Commodore Perry arrives at Uraga
1867	Emperor Meiji ascends the throne
1868–1912	*Meiji Period*
1894-95	Sino-Japanese War
1904–05	Russo–Japanese War
1910	Annexation of Korea
1912–26	*Taisho Period*
1914	Japan declares war on Germany
1915	Japan submits 21 demands to China
1923	Great Kantoh earthquake
1926 . . .	*Showa Period*
1933	Japan leaves League of Nations
1940	Tripartite treaty between Japan, Germany and Italy
1941–45	Pacific War
1945–52	Occupation of Japan by Allied forces
1946	New constitution promulgated
1952	Japan gains independence

Political system and government

Japan is a parliamentary democracy based on universal suffrage. The Emperor, being the symbol of state under the constitution, has no powers related to government. He performs only those acts stipulated in the constitution, such as appointing the Prime Minister and the Chief Justice of the Supreme Court as designated by the Diet and the Cabinet respectively, and other duties. Japan's political system, with the Diet (parliament) as the main law-making body, dates back to 1890. Then the Emperor was the source of power, but in the 1946 US-inspired constitution, sovereign power was transferred to the people and the Diet transformed from the Emperor's legislative authority to the highest organ of state power and sole law-making body.

The Diet consists of two houses: the 511-member House of Representatives and the 252-member House of Councillors. The lower House of Representatives is the stronger, and has precedence in four key areas: enactment of laws, passage of the budget, approval of treaties and choosing the Prime Minister. The House of Representatives has a four-year term, though the Prime Minister may seek a dissolution before the term is up, and House of Councillors members are elected for six-year terms with half the seats filled by election every three years.

The main political party is the Liberal Democratic Party (LDP), which has ruled ever since it was formed in November 1955 through the merger of two conservative parties. Opposition parties include Japan Socialist Party, the *Komeito* (clean government party), the Democratic Socialist Party, the Japan Communist Party, the New Liberal Club and the United Social Democratic Party. Under the Liberal Democratic constitution the party president (who is normally the Prime Minister by virtue of the party's majority) enjoys a two-year term and after two years cannot stand again, though efforts are being made to remove this restriction.

By law the administration consists of the Prime Minister's Office and 12 ministries: Justice; Foreign Affairs; Finance; Education; Health and Welfare; Agriculture, Forestry and Fisheries; International Trade and Industry; Transport; Post and Telecommunications; Labour; Construction; and Home Affairs.

In spite of being an island state with a common language and common history reinforced by centuries of isolation, Japan's political leadership has not been as strong as constant LDP rule would suggest. The ruling party is split into factions under individual leaders. Yasuhiro Nakasone, Prime Minister since 1982 and the first man for more than a decade to serve for more than a two-year term, is not the leader of the largest faction. Indeed, the real power broker of Japanese politics has been Kakuei Tanaka, forced out as Prime Minister for accepting bribes in the Lockheed scandal. The faction system means that a Japanese cabinet is not as strong as a European government cabinet: some powerful figures are excluded because they are from the wrong faction or even choose to stay out of government to bolster their party prospects.

Ministries

Prime Minister's Office
Sohri-fu, 1–6–1 Nagata-cho, Chiyoda-ku, Tokyo
(tel: 581.2361)

Ministry of Justice
Hohmu Sho, 1–1–1 Kasumigaseki, Chiyoda-ku, Tokyo
(tel: 580.4111)

Ministry of Finance
Ookura Sho, 3–1–1 Kasumigaseki, Chiyoda-ku, Tokyo
(tel: 581.4111)

Ministry of Education
Monbu Sho, 3–2–2 Kasumigaseki, Chiyoda-ku, Tokyo
(tel: 581.4211)

Ministry of Health and Welfare
Kohsei Sho, 1–2–2 Kasumigaseki, Chiyoda-ku, Tokyo
(tel: 503.1711)

Ministry of Agriculture and Forestry and Fisheries
Nohrin Suisan Sho, 1–2–1 Kasumigaseki, Chiyoda-ku,
Tokyo (tel: 502.8111)

Ministry of International Trade and Industry
Tsuusan Sho, 1–3–1 Kasumigaseki, Chiyoda-ku, Tokyo
(tel: 501.1511)

Ministry of Transport
Unyu Sho, 2–1–3 Kasumigaseki, Chiyoda-ku, Tokyo
(tel: 580.3111)

Ministry of Foreign Affairs
Gaimu Sho, 2–2–1 Kasumigaseki, Chiyoda-ku, Tokyo
(tel: 580.3311)

Ministry of Posts and Telecommunications
Yuusei Sho, 1–3–2 Kasumigaseki, Chiyoda-ku, Tokyo
(tel: 504.4411)

Ministry of Construction
Kensetsu Sho, 2–1–3 Kasumigaseki, Chiyoda-ku, Tokyo
(tel: 580.4311)

Ministry of Labour
Rohdoh Sho, 1–2–2 Kasumigaseki, Chiyoda-ku, Tokyo
(tel: 593.1211)

Ministry of Home Affairs
Jichi Sho, 2–1–2 Kasumigaseki, Chiyoda-ku, Tokyo
(tel: 581.5311)

The economy

Japan emerged from the Second World War almost literally in ashes. Not only had atomic bombs been dropped on Hiroshima and Nagasaki but the capital Tokyo had been devastated by constant US bombing raids. The main port, Yokohama, also suffered badly. Domestic stocks of goods and materials were exhausted, and inflation was a constant danger. Industrial production had plunged to 1926–27 levels, and it was estimated that it would take more than a decade for Japan to reach 1935 economic levels. Priority was given to getting basic industry started and to establishing a single exchange rate for the yen. The latter was achieved on 25 April 1949, and the yen was fixed at 360 to $1. The Korean War (June 1950 to July 1953) rescued Japan from a recession and lifted it into a boom, so that by 1956 the government could declare that the post-war period was over and growth through modernisation was the key word.

Other countries at this time failed to appreciate the great strides that Japan had made. Its fledgling efforts to export initially met with laughter in the markets of the West where the goods were considered cheap imitations of Western products of inferior quality. But the laughter did not last long. With the import of technology from the West and with their dedicated labour force the Japanese learned fast. They were not above 'dirty tricks' such as visiting Western factories taking photographs and drawings of Western processes, buying Western products and stripping them down to see exactly how they worked and then singlemindedly setting about improving and selling the improved goods back to

Selected economic indicators

	Unit	1978	1979	1980	1981	1982	1983	1984
GNP	%	9.9	8.0	7.7	6.9	5.1	3.9	6.4
Real GNP	1975 prices	5.1	5.2	4.8	4.0	3.3	3.4	5.8
Industrial production	1980 = 100	88.9	95.5	100.0	101.0	101.3	104.9	116.6
Prices – wholesale	1980 = 100	79.1	84.9	100.0	101.4	103.2	100.9	100.6
Prices – consumer	1980 = 100	89.4	92.6	100.0	104.9	107.7	109.7	112.1
Unemployment rate	%	2.1	2.1	2.0	2.2	2.4	2.6	2.7
Exports	$ bn	95.6	101.2	126.7	149.5	137.6	145.4	168.3
Imports	$ bn	71.0	99.4	124.6	129.5	119.6	114.0	124.0
Balance of trade	$ bn	24.6	1.8	2.1	19.9	18.1	31.4	44.2
Current account balance	$ bn	16.5	−8.7	−10.7	4.7	6.8	20.8	35.0
Long-term capital balance	$ bn	−12.4	−12.6	2.4	−6.4	−14.9	−17.7	−49.6
Balance of payments	$ bn	5.9	−16.6	−8.4	−2.1	−4.9	5.1	−15.2
Official reserves	$ bn	33.0	20.3	25.2	28.4	23.2	24.5	26.3

Source: Tokyo Financial Review, Sep 1985/Bank of Tokyo

the West. With a domestic market of more than 100m people – bigger than that of any Western country apart from the US – the Japanese had a homogeneous market base for testing new products.

With a dedicated labour force and company union structure, ensuring one trade union per factory (the enterprise union system), Japan has avoided the labour troubles, work stoppages and strikes common in the West. Critics accuse Japan of 'dumping' its goods on Western markets – that is, deliberately selling exports at lower prices than similar domestic products in order to gain a market share and defeat foreign competition.

Japan's discipline allowed it to survive the 'oil shocks' of 1970 and to emerge as the world's strongest economy in the 1980s. One of the most notable facts is that Japan has few resources of its own: it imports all of its oil, most of its coal and other essential raw materials. Yet in spite of having to import such material, by the 1980s Japan had a trade surplus that topped $50bn in 1985, and a surplus on the current account of about $45bn, thus beating the previous record held by Saudi Arabia ($42bn) at the height of the oil boom. Economic growth has slowed from the 10 per cent a year achieved over the twenty years before the oil crisis, but it is still 4–5 per cent a year. Critics contend that Japan is capable of 5 or 6 per cent or more a year, but this would depend on new policy initiatives and reflation which the government is loathe to embark upon.

Japan's economic structure is unique. Its industry is highly competitive and efficient, but the country also includes sectors (notably, farming, distribution and some service sectors) that are notoriously costly and inefficient. Primary industry contributes a mere 3–4 per cent to GNP, but farmers are protected from foreign imports which might damage the prices of their goods. Rice prices in Japan are two to three times higher than world market prices. The reason why farmers are pampered is that the rural areas customarily support the Liberal Democratic Party, ensuring its comfortable majority in the Diet.

The service sector is similarly inefficient because of layers of distribution network. All this means that food prices in Japan are among the highest in the world, and Japanese families spend more of their income on food than do their US or European counterparts.

Japanese industry, however, is the most competitive in the world. Japan is now the leader in electrical and electronic appliances. Automobile factories are not yet the biggest, but they are highly profitable and make use of the latest automation and robotisation techniques. Robotics is another area where Japan leads the world. Machine tools are a growing industry. In semiconductors and computers Japan is challenging what was previously thought to be an unchallengeable US lead. Japan has ambitious plans for creation of so-called fifth generation computers and artificial intelligence. The country also has a fledgling aircraft industry which in 1985 turned out its first all-Japanese jet aircraft and also has a budding space programme.

A controversial key part in building up these industries, as well as their predecessors such as shipbuilding and steel (in which Japan is the biggest and second biggest, respectively, after the Soviet Union), has been played by the Ministry of International Trade and Industry (MITI). Foreign critics allege that MITI set targets and then co-ordinated the national effort to take on and defeat the rest of the world. Another important industry is precision machinery, which includes watches and cameras, in which intensely competitive companies like Asahi Optical, Minolta, Nikon, Canon and Olympus push forward with innovations. The Japanese pharmaceutical industry is investing heavily in R&D efforts. The construction industry employs 10 per cent of the labour force but is vulnerable to economic fluctuations.

A unique feature of the Japanese industrial scene is that the final production of big companies like Toyota or Nissan is actually built up from the products of smaller companies and part-makers, some of which are as small as family workshops. More than 50 per cent of the Japanese employed in manufacturing work at plants with fewer than 100 employees.

Tertiary industries account for a large chunk of Japan's GDP. Those with growth potential include the software industry and other information industries; leasing services, restaurant chains, international banking, consumer financing and the leisure industry.

Along with its high growth Japan has enjoyed low rates of inflation and of unemployment. The employment system is traditionally based on lifetime employment and seniority-based wages, but this is changing. Bigger companies will not lay off workers but cut down on their overtime in difficult periods.

The Outlook and Guidelines for Japan's Economy in the Eighties (Apr 1983 to Mar 1990) is the tenth post-war programme to be announced. It sets out to aim for an average annual growth rate of 4 per cent in real terms and 6–7 per cent in nominal terms. This growth should broaden employment opportunities, and 2 per cent is the unemployment rate target. A 3 per cent average annual rise in consumer prices over the period is another projection.

Trade

Booming trade surpluses brought anger from the rest of the world and claims that Japan unfairly protects its markets when the government in Tokyo protested that it had fewer tariff barriers than any other industrial state, and angry critics claim that non-tariff barriers such as cumbersome customs and inspection procedures and rigorous health and safety laws plus a xenophobic attitude against foreign products kept out imports. In 1985 an increasing issue became the value of the Japanese currency, trading at about ¥250 to the US dollar, which economists reckoned was too low. After finance ministers of the five big powers met in New York in September 1985, concerted action pushed the yen towards the 200 level, which should start to give American products the chance of competition with Japanese goods.

A cause of controversy was the refusal of the Japanese Government to reflate the economy and thus raise the growth rate. Though the economic infrastructure is good (roads, railways and ports), the social and welfare system is poor. Japanese were criticised in an EEC report for living in 'rabbit hutches' because their homes were so small. The pension system is still poor. Japan also lacks parks and other social and leisure amenities, but the government has hesitated to increase spending because it is already in deficit and is fearful of raising taxes. Most of the Japanese deficit is owed to Japanese – unlike the American deficit, a large chunk of which is owed to foreigners.

Banking

Japan's financial system is heavily regulated, though a process of careful deregulation is being undertaken. There are several classes of banks, including 12 city banks plus the Bank of Tokyo, a specialised foreign exchange bank, three long-term credit banks, seven trust banks and a host of savings and regional banks. There is also the Post Office Savings Bank which has assets of more than $300bn (or twice as much as those of Citibank, the world's largest commercial bank). More than 100 foreign banks have branches in Japan but the share of all the foreigners combined is about 3 per cent of the assets.

Traditionally, Japanese banks have helped to fund the great growth of the big corporations, but from 1975 onwards corporations reduced their borrowing programme with savings rates of more than 20 per cent in net terms.

Stockmarket

Japan has the second biggest stockmarket in the world with more than 2000 companies quoted on the various markets, the most important of which is Tokyo. If Tokyo continues to grow at the same rate as it recently has it will even surpass the New York market in size.

The eight stock exchanges are in Tokyo, Osaka, Nagoya and five other major cities.

In terms of market capitalisation, the very biggest companies are banks, an unusual feature in world terms. The banks were once the centrepieces of the huge pre-war *zaibatsu* conglomerates, dismantled by the American occupying forces, but informal relationships still remain between the big companies that bear the same name: for example Mitsui, Mitsubishi and Sumitomo. In the post-war world large new companies have sprung up which include Toyota, the automobile giant, Honda Motors, Sony and Matsushita electronics concerns, Sharp, Canon and Nikon, Fujitsu, the computer concern, Hitachi and NEC, all of them are challenging world leaders if not already leaders.

Law

The Japanese judiciary is an independent branch of government with powers equal to those of the legislative and executive branches. The judicial system comprises three major parts: the courts, headed by the Supreme Court; the Public Prosecutor's Offices set up in correspondence to the courts; and Nichibenren (the Japanese Federation of Bar Associations), a private organisation. Japan has comparatively few lawyers, only about 11,000 in all. One reason for this is that the Japanese do not like going to litigation and would far rather settle matters amicably. This means that contested cases may take a lot of time, and in the commercial field it is hard to get a favourable judgement, especially for foreigners.

International fairs

Apr 1986: 17th Osaka International Trade Fair, held every other year.

Oct 1986: '86 Nishinippon International Foods & Gifts Fair, held every three years.

Oct 1986: 13th Japan International Machine Tool Fair, Osaka, held every four years.

Nov 1986: International Design Fair, Kanazawa.

Dec 1986: World Travel Fair, Tokyo, held every other year.

▦ Living there

Employment regulations

Applications for business visas and residence permits must be made before entry to Japan. Japanese consulate staff give guidance as to procedure.

Alien registration

All foreigners, with the exception of those in diplomatic service, must register at their local ward, city or village office within 90 days of arrival in Japan if they intend to remain longer than this period. For registration, the applicant must bring his/her passport plus two recent passport-type photos. Persons permitted to stay in Japan for more than one year must be fingerprinted. The alien registration certificate is valid for five years and must be carried at all times. It must be renewed 30 days prior to its expiration.

Children under 16 years need not submit photos nor be fingerprinted, and are excused from carrying the alien registration certificate. Application for renewal must be made within 30 days after the child's sixteenth birthday. Foreigners who have obtained a re-entry permit must take the certificate of alien registration with them when leaving Japan and show it to immigration inspectors on departure and entry. Those leaving Japan permanently must surrender the certificate when departing.

Taxation

Japan's tax laws require that income tax be withheld from salaries paid to individuals including foreigners. Each year between 16 Feb and 15 Mar the payee must file a return for the preceding year at the taxation office of the district where he/she resides. Failure to do so may lead to imprisonment. All taxpayers in Japan, nationals or foreigners, are subject to a local resident's tax, which is based on one's income for the preceding year. This tax is paid to the local civic office.

For taxation purposes foreigners are classified into 'permanent resident' (those who have lived in Japan continuously for over five years); 'non-permanent resident' (fewer than five years and not intending to remain permanently); and 'non-resident'. Permanent residents must declare all income, including that from or paid abroad. Non-permanent residents must declare all income paid in Japan, but not that paid abroad. Non-residents need only declare income earned in Japan.

Tax deductions
Individuals in certain business categories are entitled to tax deductions for various reasons (found in the English explanation of the tax forms published by the government).

Students
Students who work part-time and earn less than ¥330,000 a year need not file a tax return.

Arrival or departure from Japan
Foreigners who arrived in Japan the preceding year and had a total income of less than ¥330,000 need not file a return. When terminating residence in Japan, foreigners should either appoint someone to manage their tax affairs, or pay any remaining resident's tax and file an income tax statement prior to departure.

The local tax office can give information about income tax returns. Questions may also be addressed to:

Foreign Section, Tokyo Regional Taxation Bureau,
Oote-machi Dai-ni Godo Bldg, 1–3–2 Oote-machi,
Chiyoda-ku, Tokyo (tel: 216.6811, ext. 2695 or 3216).

Accommodation
Because of the congestion in the cities, rents in Japan, and especially in Tokyo, are among the highest in the world. If you want comfort in the Western style and size you must pay for it. Flats usually come with most appliances, for minimum two-year terms. There are a number of real estate agencies where English is spoken and which efficiently handle all matters relating to renting a flat. In a central area of Tokyo a three-bedroom flat could go for ¥300,000 or ¥500,000 upwards per month. It is important to specify exactly what you are looking for: proximity to schools, shopping area, public transport.

Payment of bills
Utilities bills are entirely in Japanese apart from the numbers. You can get a direct debit facility from a Japanese bank. Otherwise you may pay your bills at the post office or any Japanese bank.

Education
Japan's academic year begins in Apr and ends in Mar. Primary and junior high school education are compulsory. Primary school starts from age 6 to 12; junior high from age 13 to 15. High school, which is

optional, lasts three more years, and college four years.

There are also nursery schools and kindergartens. Foreign children may attend public nursery schools and kindergartens. Any local ward office will accept enrolment applications. These charge standard tuition fees.

Foreign parents who wish their children to attend public primary and junior high school should apply to the local civic office by October the preceding year. It helps if the children know some Japanese, though it is not essential that they speak it fluently. Public primary and junior high school are free.

Foreign children who have completed the compulsory nine years of primary and junior high school education may sit the entrance exam for high school. The examination is in Japanese and covers social studies, mathematics, science and English. Parents wishing to send their children to a public high school should consult with the Department of Senior High School Education of the Tokyo Metropolitan Government by December the preceding year.

There are a large number of private schools of international affiliations in Japan, and these should be consulted for further information.

Health

Japan is a safe country. All food factories, bottling plants, etc. are subject to rigorous sanitary and hygiene laws. Tap-water is safe to drink anywhere in Japan. Below are listed some English-speaking hospitals.

Tokyo
St Luke's International Hospital
10 Akashi-cho 1-chome, Chuo-ku, Tokyo
(tel: 541.5151)

International Catholic Hospital
2–5–1 Naka-Ochiai, Shinjuku-ku, Tokyo
(tel: 951.1111)

Tokyo Sanitarium Hospital
3–17–3 Amanuma, Suginami-ku, Tokyo
(tel: 392.6151)

Japan Red Cross Medical Centre
4–1–22 Hiroo, Shibuya-ku, Tokyo (tel: 400.1311)

Yokohama
International Goodwill Hospital
55 Aioi-cho 3-chome, Naka-ku, Yokohama (tel: 681.0221)

Red Cross Hospital
Negishi-machi, Naka-ku, Yokohama (tel: 622.0101)

Keiyu Hospital
Yamashita-cho, Naka-ku, Yokohama (tel: 651.0261)

Osaka
Yodogawa Christian Hospital
9–2–6 Awaji-higashi, Yodogawa-ku, Osaka
(tel: 322.2250)

Red Cross Hospital
5–3 Tennohji-ku, Fudegasaki, Osaka (tel: 771.5131)

A good medical insurance cover ought to help with bills, so it is advisable to get one before coming to Japan, or arrange it as soon as you arrive.

Shopping
All labels, instructions on goods and in supermarkets, etc. are in Japanese. It is a good idea to get a Japanese friend or your maid to go shopping with you to point out the whereabouts of various goods so that you get exactly what you want. Some supermarkets in Tokyo that cater for Western tastes are listed below:

Benten
102 Wakamatsu-cho, Shinjuku (tel: 202.2421)
They deliver and have low prices

Hara Store
Azabu-Juuban, near Ichinohashi (tel: 451.5211)
They deliver

Meijiya
2–2–8 Kyobashi, Chuo-ku (tel: 271.1111)
Has branches in Ginza and Roppongi

National Azabu
4–5–2 Minami-Azabu, Minato-ku (tel: 442.3181)
Mostly imported foods and unusual items, good liquor and wine. Phone orders accepted. Delivery service

Olympia Foodliner
6-35-3 Jingumae, Shibuya-ku (tel: 400.7351)

Yours
3–5–12 Kita-Aoyama, Minato-ku (tel: 408.6101)
Low prices; stays open till 0200

Almost all Western supermarkets will accept a personal yen cheque.

Department stores
Daimaru
1–9–1 Marunouchi, Chiyoda-ku. Closed on Wed. Branch in Osaka

Hankyu
5–2–1 Ginza, Chuo-ku. Closed on Thur. Branches in Yurakucho and Osaka

Isetan
3–14–1 Shinjuku, Shinjuku-ku. Closed Wed. Has a selection of Western clothes in foreign sizes

Keio
1–1–4 Nishi-Shinjuku, Shinjuku-ku. Closed on Thur

Matsuya
3–6–1 Ginza, Chuo-ku. Closed on Thur

Matsuzakaya
6–10–1 Ginza, Chuo-ku. Closed on Wed. Branches in Ueno and Osaka

Mitsukoshi
1–7–4 Nihonbashi Muro-machi, Chuo-ku. Closed on Mon. Branches in Yokohama and Osaka as well as Ginza, and Shinjuku. The largest department store in Japan

Odakyu
1–1–3 Nishi-Shinjuku, Shinjuku-ku. Closed on Thur

Seibu
1–28–1 Minami-Ikebukuro, Toshima-ku. Closed on Wed. Also in Shibuya

Sogo
1–11–1 Yuuraku-cho, Chiyoda-ku. Closed on Thur. Branch in Osaka

Takashimaya
2–4–1 Nihonbashi, Chuo-ku. Closed on Wed. Branches in Tamagawa, Yokohama and Osaka

Tokyu
2–24–1 Dohgenzaka, Shibuya-ku. Closed on Thur. Branch in Nihonbashi

Cost of living
Japan is very expensive. Remember that the Japanese spend more on their food bills than their European or American counterparts. That should say it all.

Entertainment
There are theatres, cinemas and clubs in Tokyo, Osaka and Yokohama. Each city has its own downtown night spots, for the Japanese are fond of an evening on the town. Traditional geisha houses, modern night-clubs and numerous bars provide evening entertainment. During the day there are always exhibitions and expositions worth going to. Amusement arcades with TV games and *pachinko* parlours abound.

Worship
There are a number of religious denominations in Japan, all free to coexist.

Leisure
There are a number of sports centres in Japan. Popular sports include baseball, the martial arts, skiing, skating, swimming, golf.

Among family clubs are the American Club and the Yokohama Country and Athletic Club.

Newspapers

There are four English-language dailies: the *Mainichi Daily News;* the *Japan Times; Asahi Evening News* and the *Daily Yomiuri.*

A variety of regional business newspapers are also available, as are the *Asian Wall Street Journal* and the *International Herald Tribune* and overseas editions of other magazines and newspapers. The *Japan Economic Journal* is a financial weekly. The most influential Japanese-language financial paper is the *Nihon Keizai Shinbun.*

Earthquake precautions

A very important feature of Japanese life is the ever-present fear of another earthquake. Obviously, construction has been modified to minimise earthquake shocks. However, in the event of an earthquake follow the instructions posted in your hotel room. If you are near the seashore, move away quickly when the quake stops before the tidal wave arrives. If you are at home, turn off all electricity and gas mains and take shelter. Many Japanese keep a ready-packed kit near the front door, with torch, first-aid kit and other necessities.

Posts and telecommunications

There are post offices all over the major cities. The telecommunication infrastructure is efficient. Public telephone call boxes are coloured green, blue, red and yellow. A local call costs ¥10 per 30 seconds. International direct dialling boxes are green. Area codes always start with 0; Tokyo is 03, Osaka 06, Yokohama 045, Narita 0476.

There are 24-hour KDD (Kokusai Denshin Denwa) offices handling telegrams, facsimiles and phototelegrams, with booths for ISD calls and telex in Tokyo.

Tokyo Telegraph Office
1–8–1 Oote-machi, Tokyo
(tel: 211.5588)

Osaka Telegraph Office
1–25 Bingo-machi, Higashi-ku, Osaka
(tel: 288.2151).

? Directory

Useful business addresses

Federation of Economic Organisations (Keidanren)
Keidanren Kaikan
1–9–4 Oote-machi, Chiyoda-ku, Tokyo
(tel: 279.141)
Kansai office: Osaka Bldg, 3–6–32 Nakanoshima, Kita-ku
Osaka (tel: 441.0841)

Japan Committee for Economic Development
1–4–6 Marunouchi, Chiyoda-ku, Tokyo
(tel: 211.1271)

Japan Management Association
Nihon Noritsu Kyokai Bldg, 3–1–22 Shibakoen, Minato-ku,
Tokyo
(tel: 434.6211)
Osaka office: 2–30 Azuchi-machi, Higashi-ku, Osaka
(tel: 261.7151)

**Japan National Committee of the International Chamber of
Commerce**
Tokyo Kaijo Bldg, 1–2–1 Marunouchi, Chiyoda-ku, Tokyo
(tel: 213.8585)

Japan External Trade Organisation
2–2–5 Toranomon, Minato-ku, Tokyo
(tel: 582.5511)

Japan Foreign Trade Council Inc.
World Trade Centre Bldg, 6th floor, 2–4–1
Hamamatsu-cho, Minato-ku, Tokyo
(tel: 435.5952)

Japan Federation of Importers Organisation
Nihonbashi Daiwa Bldg, 1–6–1 Nihonbashi Hon-cho,
Chuo-ku, Tokyo
(tel: 270.2020)

Japan Commercial Arbitration Association
Tohsho Bldg, 3–2–2 Marunouchi, Chiyoda-ku, Tokyo
(tel: 214.0641)

Japan Chamber of Commerce and Industry
3–2–2 Marunouchi, Chiyoda-ku, Tokyo
(tel: 283.7500)

Tokyo Chamber of Commerce and Industry
3–2–2 Marunouchi, Chiyoda-ku, Tokyo
(tel: 283.7610)

Osaka Chamber of Commerce and Industry
58–7 Uchihon-machi, Hashizume-cho, Higashi-ku, Osaka
(tel: 944.6412)

Yokohama Chamber of Commerce and Industry
2 Yamashita-cho, Naka-ku, Yokohama
(tel: 671.7411)

Useful telephone numbers:

Police	110
Fire/Ambulance	119
Time	117
Weather	177
International operator	0051
Directory (central Tokyo)	104
Directory (outside central Tokyo)	105
Directory (overseas)	KDD Tokyo 270.5111
	KDD Osaka 228.2300
Tokyo events (English)	503.2911

Forwarding/clearing agents

CTI World Trade Corp
Sanno Grand Bldg, 4th floor, 2–14–2 Nagata-cho,
Chiyoda-ku, Tokyo (tel: 03.581.9711)

Fracht Fwo Ltd
Rm 601 Minatoya Bldg, 3–11–8 Shibaura, Minato-ku,
Tokyo (tel: 03.798.1601)

Kintetsu World Express Inc
Time & Life Bldg, 2–3–6 Oote-machi, Chiyoda-ku, Tokyo
(tel: 03.270.7251)

Kuehne & Nagel (Japan) Ltd
3–8–6 Nihonbashi, Hama-cho, Chuo-ku, Tokyo
(tel: 03.669.3081)
Matsuhara Bldg 1F-E, 4–2–10 Minami Horie, Nishi-ku,
Osaka (tel: 06.353.4182)

Isewan-Pracht International Ltd
A-1 Bldg, 8–2 Taiyuji-cho, Kita-ku, Osaka
(tel: 06.315.8772)

Japan Express
1–1 Kaigan-doori, Naka-ku, Yokohama
(tel: 045.211.1221)

Couriers

DHL Japan Ltd
38 Kowa Bldg, 5th floor, 4–12–24 Nishi-Azabu, Minato-ku,
Tokyo
(tel: 03.499.4811)
1–1–2 Hotarugaike Nishi-machi, Toyonaka, Osaka
(tel: 06.844.1287)

Federal Express (Japan) KK
Shin-Tokyo Bldg, 3–3–1 Marunouchi, Chiyoda-ku, Tokyo
(tel: 03.201.4331)

Overseas Courier Service
9 Shibaura 2-chome, Minato-ku, Tokyo
(tel: 03.453.8311)
3–1–14 Nosato, Nishi-Yodogawa-ku, Osaka
(tel: 06.473.2631)

TNT Skypak Japan Inc
5–5–5 Konan, Minato-ku, Toyko
(tel: 03.474.8781)

Diplomatic representation

Australia
Australian Embassy
2–1–14 Mita, Minato-ku, Tokyo 108
(tel: 453.0251/9)

Australian Consulate-General
(Osaka) Kokusai Bldg, 2–30 Azuchi-machi, Higashi-ku,
Osaka 541
(tel: 271.7071)

Austria
Embassy of the Republic of Austria
1–1–20 Moto-Azabu, Minato-ku, Tokyo 106
(tel: 451.8281/3)

Bangladesh
Embassy of the People's Republic of Bangladesh
2–7–45 Shirogane, Minato-ku, Tokyo 108
(tel: 442.1501/2)

Canada
Embassy of Canada
7–3–38 Akasaka, Minato-ku, Tokyo 107
(tel: 408.2101/8)

China
Embassy of the People's Republic of China
3–4–33 Moto-Azabu, Minato-ku, Tokyo 106
(tel: 403.3380)

Consulate-General of the People's Republic of China
4–7–1 Kami-Shinden, Toyonaka, Osaka 565
(tel: 834.0151)

Denmark
Royal Danish Embassy
29–6 Sarugaku-cho, Shibuya-ku, Tokyo 150
(tel: 496.3001)

Fiji
Embassy of Fiji
Noa Bldg, 10th floor, 2–3–5 Azabudai, Minato-ku,
Tokyo 106 (tel: 587.2038)

Finland
Embassy of Finland
3–5–39 Minami Azabu, Minato-ku, Tokyo 106
(tel: 442.2231)

France
French Embassy
4–11–44 Minami-Azabu, Minato-ku, Tokyo 106
(tel: 473.0171/9)

Consulate-General of France
Iyo Bldg, 4–41 Minami-Hon-machi, Higashi-ku, Osaka 541
(tel: 252.5995)

Germany
Embassy of the Federal Republic of Germany
4–5–10 Minami-Azabu, Minato-ku, Tokyo 106
(tel: 473.0151/7)

Consulate-General of the Federal Republic of Germany
(Osaka/Kobe) Kobe Kokusai Kaikan, 8–1–6 Goko-dori,
Chuo-ku, Kobe 651
(tel: 232.1212/5)

German Democratic Republic
Embassy of the German Democratic Republic
Akasaka Mansion, 7–5–16 Akasaka, Minato-ku, Tokyo 107
(tel: 585.5401/7)

India
Embassy of India
2–2–11 Kudan-minami, Chiyoda-ku, Tokyo 100
(tel: 262.2391/7)

Indonesia
Embassy of the Republic of Indonesia
5–2–9 Higashi-Gotanda, Shinagawa-ku, Tokyo 141
(tel: 441.4201)

Ireland
Embassy of Ireland
25 Kowa Bldg, 8–7 Sanban-cho, Chiyoda-ku, Tokyo 102
(tel: 263.0695)

Italy
Embassy of Italy
2–5–4 Mita, Minato-ku, Tokyo 108
(tel: 452.5291/6)

Honorary Consulate-General
c/o Uro Senke Osaka Branch, Nihon Bunka Kaikan, 3–41
Kitahama, Higashi-ku, Osaka 541
(tel: 231.7129)

Kiribati
Honorary Consulate of the Republic of Kiribati
Marunouchi Bldg, 2–4–1 Marunouchi, Chiyoda-ku,
Tokyo 100 (tel: 201.3487)

South Korea
Embassy of the Republic of Korea
1–2–5 Minami-Azabu, Minato-ku, Tokyo 106
(tel: 452.7611/9)

Malaysia
Embassy of Malaysia
20–16 Nanpeidai, Shibuya-ku, Tokyo 150
(tel: 463.0241/5)

Nauru
Consulate of the Republic of Nauru
Rm 122 Tokyo Club Bldg, 3–2–6 Kasumigaseki,
Chiyoda-ku, Tokyo 100
(tel: 581.9277/8)

Netherlands
Royal Netherlands Embassy
3–6–3 Shibakoen, Minato-ku, Tokyo 105
(tel: 431.5126/9)

Honorary Consulate of the Netherlands
Nedlloyd House, 25 Yamashita-cho, Naka-ku,
Yokohama 231 (tel: 651.1661)

New Zealand
New Zealand Embassy
20–40 Kamiyama-cho, Shibuya-ku, Tokyo 150
(tel: 467.2271)

Norway
Royal Norwegian Embassy
5–12–2 Minami-Azabu, Minato-ku, Tokyo 106
(tel: 440.2611)

Pakistan
Embassy of the Islamic Republic of Pakistan
2–14–9 Moto-Azabu, Minato-ku, Tokyo 106
(tel: 454.4861/4)

Papua New Guinea
Embassy of Papua New Guinea
Rm 313, Mita Kokusai Bldg, 1–4–28 Mita, Minato-ku,
Tokyo 108
(tel: 454.7801/4)

Philippines
Embassy of the Republic of the Philippines
11–24 Nanpeidai, Shibuya-ku, Tokyo 150
(tel: 496.2731/6)

Portugal
Embassy of Portugal
Olympia Annexe 304, 305, 306, 6–31–21 Jingumae,
Shibuya-ku, Tokyo 150
(tel: 400.7907)

Singapore
Embassy of the Republic of Singapore
5–12–2 Roppongi, Minato-ku, Tokyo 106
(tel: 586.9111/4)

Spain
Embassy of Spain
1–3–29 Roppongi, Minato-ku, Tokyo 106
(tel: 583.8531/2)

Sri Lanka
Embassy of the Democratic Socialist Republic of Sri Lanka
1–14–1 Akasaka, Minato-ku, Tokyo 107
(tel: 585.7431)

Sweden
Royal Swedish Embassy
1–10–3 Roppongi, Minato-ku, Tokyo 106
(tel: 582.6981/9)

Switzerland
Embassy of Switzerland
5–9–12 Minami-Azabu, Minato-ku, Tokyo 106
(tel: 473.0121)

Thailand
Royal Thai Embassy
3–14–6 Kami-Osaki, Shinagawa-ku, Tokyo 141
(tel: 441.7352)

Union of Soviet Socialist Republics
Embassy of the Union of Soviet Socialist Republics
2–1–1 Azabudai, Minato-ku, Tokyo 106
(tel: 583.4224)

United Kingdom
Her Britannic Majesty's Embassy
1 Ichiban-cho, Chiyoda-ku, Tokyo 102
(tel: 265.5511)

British Consulate-General
Hongkong Shanghai Bank Bldg, 45 Awaji-cho 4-chome,
Higashi-ku, Osaka 541
(tel: 231.3355/7)

United States of America
Embasssy of the United States of America
1–10–5 Akasaka, Minato-ku, Tokyo 107
(tel: 583.7141)

American Consulate-General
Sankei Bldg, 2–4–9 Umeda-machi, Kita-ku, Osaka 530
(tel: 341.2754/9)

Taiwan
Association of East Asian Relations
(Formerly Embassy of the Rep. of China)
Heiwadoh Bldg, 2nd floor–4th floor, 1–8–7 Higashi Azabu,
Minato-ku, Tokyo 106
(tel: 583.2171/5)
Asahi Seimei Bldg, 2nd floor, 60 Nihon Oodoori, Naka-ku,
Yokohama 231
(tel: 641.7737/8)
Nichiei Bldg, 4th floor, 1–4–8 Tosabori, Nishi-ku,
Osaka 550 (tel: 443.8481/6)

Banks

Central bank
Bank of Japan
2–2–1 Hongoku-cho, Chuo-ku, Tokyo
(tel: 03.729.1111; tx: 22763)

City banks
Dai-Ichi Kangyo Bank
1–1–5 Uchisaiwai-cho, Chiyoda-ku, Tokyo 100
(tel: 03.596.1111; tx: 22315)

Daiwa Bank
2–21 Bingo-machi, Higashi-ku, Osaka 541
(tel: 06.271.1221; tx: 63284)

Fuji Bank
1–5–5 Oote-machi, Chiyoda-ku, Tokyo 100
(tel: 03.216.2211; tx: 22367)

Hokkaido Takushoku Bank
3–7 Oodori-nishi, Chuo-ku, Sapporo 060
(tel: 011.271.2111; tx: 22801)

Kyowa Bank
1–1–2 Oote-machi, Chiyoda-ku, Tokyo 100
(tel: 03.287.2111; tx: 24275)

Mitsubishi Bank
2–7–1 Marunouchi, Chiyoda-ku, Tokyo 100
(tel: 03.240.1111; tx: 22358)

Mitsui Bank
1–1–2 Yuuraku-cho, Chiyoda-ku, Tokyo 100
(tel: 03.501.1111; tx: 22378)

Saitama Bank
7–4–1 Tokiwa, Urawa, Saitama Pref. 336
(tel: 0488.24.2411; tx: 22811)
1–3–1 Kyobashi, Chuo-ku, Tokyo 104 (tel: 03.276.6611)

Sanwa Bank
4–10 Fushimi-machi, Higashi-ku, Osaka 541
(tel: 06.202.2281; tx: 63234)

Sumitomo Bank
5–22 Kitahama, Higashi-ku, Osaka 541
(tel: 06.227.2111; tx: 63266)

Taiyo Kohbe Bank
56 Naniwa-cho, Chuo-ku, Kobe
(tel: 078.331.8101; tx: 78823)

Tohkai Bank
3–21–24 Nishiki, Naka-ku, Nagoya 460
(tel: 052.211.1111; tx: 59947)

Bank of Tokyo
1–6–3 Nihonbashi, Hongoku-cho, Chuo-ku, Tokyo 103
(tel: 03.245.1111; tx: 22220)

Long-term credit banks
Industrial Bank of Japan
1–3–3 Marunouchi, Chiyoda-ku, Tokyo 100
(tel: 03.214.1111; tx: 22325)

Long-term Credit Bank of Japan
1–2–4 Oote-machi, Chiyoda-ku, Tokyo 100
(tel: 03.211.5111; tx: 24308)

Nippon Credit Bank
1–13–10 Kudan-kita, Chiyoda-ku, Tokyo 102
(tel: 03.263.1111; tx: 26921)

Trust banks
Chuo Trust and Banking
1–7–1 Kyobashi, Chuo-ku, Tokyo
(tel: 03.567.1451; tx: 23368)

Mistsui Trust and Banking
2–1–1 Nihonbashi, Muro-machi, Chuo-ku, Tokyo
(tel: 03.270.9511; tx: 26397)

Mitsubishi Trust and Banking
Eiraku Bldg, 1–4–5 Marunouchi, Chiyoda-ku, Tokyo
(tel: 03.212.1211; tx: 24259)

Nippon Trust and Banking
3–1–8 Nihonbashi, Chuo-ku, Tokyo
(tel: 03.272.1261; tx: 24197)

Sumitomo Trust and Banking
2–3–1 Yaesu, Chuo-ku, Tokyo
(tel: 03.286.1111; tx: 28631)

Tohyo Trust and Banking
1–4–3 Marunouchi, Chiyoda-ku, Tokyo
(tel: 03.287.2211; tx: 22123)

Yasuda Trust and Banking
1–2–1 Yaesu, Chuo-ku, Tokyo
(tel: 03.278.8111; tx: 23720)

Airline offices

Tokyo
Aer Lingus
Yamaga Bldg, 1–10–9 Azabudai, Minato-ku, Tokyo
(tel: 582.8886)

Aeroflot Soviet Air Lines
Tatsunuma Bldg, 1–3–19 Yaesu, Chuo-ku
(tel: 272.5311)

Aerolineas Argentinas
33 Mori Bldg, 2nd floor, 3–8–21 Toranomon, Minato-ku
(tel: 433.1195)

Air Canada
New Akasaka Bldg, 3–2–3 Akasaka, Minato-ku
(tel: 586.3891)

Air France
Shin Aoyama Bldg, Nishi-kan 15th floor, 1–1–1 Minami
Aoyama, Minato-ku
(tel: 475.2211)

Air-India
Hibiya Park Bldg, 1–8–1 Yuuraku-cho, Chiyoda-ku
(tel: 214.7631)

Air Nauru
Tokyo Club Bldg, 3–2–6 Kasumigaseki, Chiyoda-ku
(tel: 581.9271)

Air New Zealand
Shin Kokusai Bldg, 3–4–1 Marunouchi Chiyoda-ku
(tel: 287.1641)

Air Lanka
Dowa Bldg, 1st floor, 7–2–22 Ginza, Chuo-ku
(tel: 573.4261)

Alitalia Airline
Tokyo Club Bldg, 3–2–6 Kasumigaseki, Chiyoda-ku
(tel: 580.2175)

Bangladesh Bimah
Kasumigaseki Bldg, 3rd floor, 3-2-5 Kasumigaseki,
Chiyoda-ku
(tel: 593.1252)

British Airways
Hibiya Park Bldg, 1-8-1 Yuuraku-cho, Chiyoda-ku
(tel: 214.4161)

Canadian Pacific Airlines
Hibiya Park Bldg, 1-8-1 Yuuraku-cho, Chiyoda-ku
(tel: 212.5811)

Cathay Pacific Airways Ltd
1-5-2 Yuuraku-cho, Chiyoda-ku
(tel: 504.1531)

China Airlines
Matsuoka Bldg, 5-22-10 Shinbashi, Minato-ku
(tel: 436.1501)

Civil Aviation of China
3-4-38 Moto-Azabu, Minato-ku
(tel: 404.3711)

Continental Airlines
Rm 517, Sanno Grand Bldg, 2-14-2 Nagata-cho,
Chiyoda-ku
(tel: 592.1731)

Egyptair
Palace Bldg, 1-1-1 Marunouchi, Chiyoda-ku
(tel: 211.4525)

Finnair
Gadelius Bldg, 1-7-8 Moto-Akasaka, Minato-ku
(tel: 423.0423)

Garuda Indonesian Airways
Rm 1518, Kasumigaseki Bldg, 3-2-5 Kasumigaseki,
Chiyoda-ku
(tel: 593.1181)

Iran Air
Akasaka Habitation Bldg, 1-3-5 Akasaka, Minato-ku
(tel: 586.2101)

Iraqi Airways
Akasaka Matsudaira Bldg, 3-4-1 Akasaka, Minato-ku
(tel: 586.5801)

Japan Air Lines
Dai-ni Tekko Bldg, 1-8-2 Marunouchi, Chiyoda-ku
(tel: 457.1111/456.2111)

Japan Asia Airways
Yuuraku-cho Denki Bldg S-2F, 1-7-1 Yuuraku-cho,
Chiyoda-ku (tel: 284.2666)

KLM Royal Dutch Airlines
Yuuraku-cho Denki bldg, 1-7-1 Yuuraku-cho, Chiyoda-ku
(tel: 216.0761)

Korean Airlines
Shin Kokusai Bldg, 3-4-1 Marunouchi, Chiyoda-ku
(tel: 211.3361)

Lufthansa German Airlines
Tokyo Club Bldg, 3–2–6 Kasumigaseki, Chiyoda-ku
(tel: 580.2121)

Northwest Airlines
5–12–12 Toranomon, Minato-ku
(tel: 433.8151)

Pakistan International Airlines
214 Yuuraku-cho Bldg, 1–10–1 Yuuraku-cho, Chiyoda-ku
(tel: 216.4641)

Pan American World Airways
Kokusai Bldg, 3–1–1 Marunouchi, Chiyoda-ku
(tel: 240.8888)

Philippine Airlines
Sanno Grand Bldg, 8th floor, 2–14–2 Nagata-cho,
Chiyoda-ku (tel: 580.1571)

Qantas Airways Ltd
Tokyo Chamber of Commerce Bldg, 3–2–2 Marunouchi,
Chiyoda-ku
(tel: 211.4481)

Sabena Belgian Airlines
2–2–19 Akasaka, Minato-ku
(tel: 585.6651)

Scandinavian Airlines
Toho Twin Tower Bldg, 1–5–2 Yuuraku-cho, Chiyoda-ku
(tel: 503.3151)

Singapore Airlines
Yuuraku-cho Bldg, 7th floor, 1–10–1 Yuuraku-cho,
Chiyoda-ku
(tel: 213.3431)

Swissair
Hibiya Park Bldg, 1–8–1 Yuuraku-cho, Chiyoda-ku
(tel: 212.1011)

Thai Airways International
Asahi Seimei Hibiya Bldg, 1–5–1 Yuuraku-cho, Chiyoda-ku
(tel: 503.3311)

Toa Domestic Airlines
18 Mori Bldg, 2–3–13 Toranomon, Minato-ku
(tel: 507.8030)

United Airlines
Suite 228 Kokusai Bldg, 3–1–1 Marunouchi, Chiyoda-ku
(tel: 213.4511)

UTA French Airlines
Kasumigaseki Bldg, 33rd floor, 3–2–5 Kasumigaseki,
Chiyoda-ku (tel: 593.0771)

Varig Brazilian Airlines
Palace Bldg, 1–1–1 Marunouchi, Chiyoda-ku
(tel: 211.6761)

Osaka
Air Canada
4–12 Hirano-cho, Higashi-ku
(tel: 227.1180)

Air France
Nittochi Yodoyabashi Bldg, 1 Ookawa-cho, Higashi-ku
(tel: 201.5161)

Air-India
Osaka Kokusai Bldg, 30 Azuchi-machi 2-chome,
Higashi-ku (tel: 264.5911)

Alitalia Airlines
Nishi Hansin Bldg, 2–3–24 Umeda, Kita-ku
(tel: 341.3951)

All Nippon Airways
Zennikku Bldg, 2–6–23 Shibata, Kita-ku
(tel: 372.2551)

British Airways
Suntory Bldg, 2–1–40 Dojimahama, Kita-ku
(tel: 345.2761)

Canadian Pacific Airlines
Nishi Hanshin Bldg, 2–3–24 Umeda, Kita-ku
(tel: 346.5591)

Cathay Pacific Airways
Kintetsu Hon-machi Bldg, 4–28–1 Hon-machi, Higashi-ku
(tel: 245.6731)

Civil Aviation of China
2–10–18 Uchihon-machi, Higashi-ku
(tel: 946.1702)

Egyptair
Nishi Hanshin Bldg, 2–3–24 Umeda, Kita-ku
(tel: 341.1575)

Finnair
Hon-machi Nomura Bldg, 4–4–1 Hon-machi, Higashi-ku
(tel: 261.0403)

Japan Air Lines
Asahi Shinbun Bldg, 3–2–4 Nakanoshima, Kita-ku
(tel: 203.1212/201.1231)

Japan Asia Airways
Kanase Bldg, 14 Hon-machi 4-chome, Higashi-ku
(tel: 271.7333)

KLM Royal Dutch Airlines
Shin Sakurabashi Bldg, 2–1–24 Umeda, Kita-ku
(tel: 345.6691)

Korean Air Lines
KAL Bldg, 3–12–1 Hon-machi, Higashi-ku
(tel: 262.1110)

Lufthansa German Airlines
Sakurabashi Toyo Bldg, 2–2–16 Sonezaki Shinchi, Kita-ku
(tel: 341.4885)

Northwest Airlines
Teisan Nakanoshima Bldg, 2–2–8 Nakanoshima, Kita-ku
(tel: 228.0747)

Pakistan International Airlines
Nishi-Hanshin Bldg, 2–3–24 Umeda, Kita-ku
(tel: 341.3106)

Pan American World Airways
Nomura Bldg, 4–4–1 Hon-machi, Higashi-ku
(tel: 271.3191)

Philippine Airlines
Sumitomo Nakanoshima Bldg, 2nd floor, 3–2–18
Nakanoshima, Kita-ku
(tel: 444.2541)

Qantas Airways
Osaka Kokusai Bldg, 30 Azuchi-machi 2-chome,
Higashi-ku
(tel: 262.1341)

Sabena Belgian Airlines
Nishi Hanshin Bldg, 2–3–24 Umeda, Kita-ku
(tel: 341.8081)

Scandinavian Airlines
Kintetsu Dojima Bldg, 10th floor, 2–2–2 Dojima, Kita-ku
(tel: 348.0611)

Singapore Airlines
Shin Ujiden Bldg, 1–2–6 Sonezaki, Kita-ku
(tel: 364.0881)

Swissair
Chiyoda Seimei Bldg, 35 Hirano-machi 4-chome,
Higashi-ku
(tel: 227.0831)

Thai Airways International
Sumitomo Seimei Yodoyabashi Bldg, 27 Ookawa-cho,
Higashi-ku
(tel: 202.7337)

Toa Domestic Airlines
Osaka Ekimae Daiichi Bldg, 6th floor, 1–3–1–600 Umeda,
Kita-ku
(tel: 345.7977)

UTA French Airlines
Daiko Bldg, 3–2–14 Umeda, Kita-ku
(tel: 345.0616)

Varig Brazilian Airlines
Nishi Hanshin Bldg, 2–3–24 Umeda, Kita-ku
(tel: 341.3571)

Yokohama
Air France
Daiwa Bank Bldg, 47 Onoe-cho 4-chome, Naka-ku
(tel: 641.8134)

Air-India
Kannai Nihon Bldg, 1–2 Tokiwa-cho, Naka-ku
(tel: 651.2874)

All Nippon Airways
Shin Tokiwa Bldg, 4–39 Tokiwa-cho, Naka-ku
(tel: 641.2051)

Cathay Pacific Airways
Maersk Bldg, 8th floor, 18 Nihon-Oodoori, Naka-ku
(tel: 681.5861)

Japan Air Lines
Sotetsu Bldg, 1–3–23 Kita Saiwai, Nishi-ku
(tel: 323.1911)

Lufthansa German Airlines
Utoku Bldg, 9th floor, 85 Benten-doori 6-chome, Naka-ku
(tel: 201.2570)

Scandinavian Airlines
Sangyo Boeki Centre Bldg, 2 Yamashita-cho, Naka-ku
(tel: 671.7207)

Singapore Airlines
Kannai Ekimae Daiichi Bldg, Rm 211, 12 Masago-cho
2-chome, Naka-ku
(tel: 681.7021)

Travel agents

Tokyo
Air Travel Centre Orient Travel Ltd
Rm 408, Bellza Roppongi Bldg, 4–1–9 Roppongi,
Minato-ku
(tel: 586.3371)

Dodwell Travel Service
Rm 111, Nippon Bldg, 2–6–2 Oote-machi, Chiyoda-ku
(tel: 241.8020)

Fujita Travel Service
Godo Bldg, 6–2–10 Ginza, Chuo-ku
(tel: 573.1011)

Japan Travel Bureau
1–13–1 Nihonbashi, Chuo-ku
(tel: 284.7619)

Nippon Express Co Ltd
8–11–11 Ginza, Chuo-ku
(tel: 574.1211)

Osaka
Fujita Travel Service
Shin Asahi Bldg, 2–3–18 Nakanoshima, Kita-ku
(tel: 203.3191)

Japan Travel Bureau
Osaka Umeda Office, 3–11 Umeda, Kita-ku
(tel: 344.0022)

Nippon Express Co
1–3–16 Sonezaki-Shinchi, Kita-ku
(tel: 345.1751)

Yokohama
Japan Travel Bureau
1–1–13 Kita-Saiwai, Nishi-ku
(tel: 312.2839)

Nippon Express Co
1–4–1 Kita-Saiwai, Nishi-ku
(tel: 319.5101)

Appointments and notes

Day 1

Day 2

Day 3

Day 4

Day 5

Day 6

Day 7

Appointments and notes

Day 8

Day 9

Day 10

Day 11

Day 12

Day 13

Day 14